THE
AGAINST
THE
INTELLECT

THE WAR AGAINST THE INTELLECT

Peter Shaw

EPISODES IN THE DECLINE OF DISCOURSE

UNIVERSITY OF IOWA PRESS ꝏ IOWA CITY

University of Iowa Press, Iowa City 52242
Copyright © 1989 by the University of Iowa
Printed in the United States of America
First edition, 1989

Typesetting by G&S Typesetters, Austin, Texas
Printing and binding by Thomson-Shore,
    Dexter, Michigan

Library of Congress
Cataloging-in-Publication Data
Shaw, Peter, 1936–
The war against the intellect: episodes in the
decline of discourse/by Peter Shaw.—1st ed.
    p. cm.
ISBN 0-87745-230-X, ISBN 0-87745-240-7 (pbk.)
1. United States—Intellectual life—20th
century. 2. American literature—
History and criticism—Theory, etc.
3. Criticism—United States—History—
20th century. I. Title.
E169.12.S47 1989   88-32115
973.92—dc19   CIP

TO MY SON, STEVEN

CONTENTS

ACKNOWLEDGMENTS

My thanks to the magazine editors who were willing to print my essays even though they were likely to bring letters of protest, and who in several cases helped me clarify my arguments and improve my style: George Core of *Sewanee Review*, Joseph Epstein of the *American Scholar*, Norman Podhoretz and Neal Kozodoy of *Commentary*, Hilton Kramer of the *New Criterion*, Lewis Lapham of *Harper's*, William Phillips of *Partisan Review*, and Gregory Wolfe of *Intercollegiate Review*. Thanks, too, to my personal editors, Penelope Shaw and Steven Shaw; to Susan Thompson, E. D. Hirsch, and James N. Jordan for their readings of individual essays; and to Jacques Barzun for his invaluable close scrutiny of the entire manuscript.

INTRODUCTION

The intellectual climate of our time has undergone a subtle alteration in the past twenty years. Starting in the 1960s a change came over the rules of discourse whereby the marshaling of logic and evidence gradually lost its prestige. In its place right feeling and good intentions came to reign as the highest intellectual values and the most persuasive earnests of high seriousness. It became common, for example, for writers to reassure their readers that they were particularly sensitive to the problems of ethnicity or poverty or disease or any other lamentable status or condition. The spirit of the 1960s, which favored the heart over the head, was making itself felt across the spectrum of argumentative writing and scholarship. This was the war against the intellect.

The war was never explicitly declared, nor was it perceived to be under way by the guardians of culture—scholars and intellectuals. My own realization that something had changed came after my return to teaching at the State University of New York at Stony Brook in 1970, following a year away from higher education. In response to resolutions against the Vietnam War and racism drawn up by the Black Panther Party and approved by the Yale University faculty, a faculty meeting was called at Stony Brook. The meeting took place immediately after the shootings of students at Kent State University, at a time when it was not yet clear exactly what had happened there. The overriding feeling, though, was that the Stony Brook faculty ought to issue some kind of resolution. To my surprise, with little discussion its members adopted the Black Panther resolutions despite their limited relevance to the situation at hand.

Only six or seven faculty members besides myself out of some fifteen hundred present voted against. I attempted to speak but was prevented from doing so by parliamentary maneuvering. Yet what, I have often wondered, would I have said if recognized by the chair? It would have been insulting to the intelligence of my colleagues to point out the obvious inappropriateness of the resolutions. Something unspoken in the air was leading to a positive vote, but what it might be my year away from the university had rendered me incapable of grasping. The next day when I asked a colleague to give me his view of the Panther resolutions, he frankly described them as irrelevant to our situation. He had voted for them because he shared the general feeling that something had to be done.

The thinking to which I was not yet privy appears in retrospect to have been the product of long-suffered distress over the Vietnam War, brought to a head by the shocking deaths of the Kent State students. In the circumstances it was taken as self-evident by all but six or seven faculty members that reason should be set aside. Henceforth, as it developed, the willed suspension of the critical faculty in the service of a perceived cause or higher principle would come to be regarded as a mark of intellectual distinction. As this attitude seeped into the intellectual process, scholarship and intellectual discourse were invaded by what might be called theories of feeling and personal experience. It was first asserted by a few and eventually accepted by many that the capacity to reason on a subject was less valuable than the bringing to bear of one's political convictions, one's gender experience, or one's social status (or, rather, an attitude toward social status).

⤜ A virtually automatic suspension of the rules of proof, reason, and logic was now accorded to certain privileged kinds of discourse: the championing of artistic works by those newly designated as minorities or the oppressed; accusations of Western historical guilt toward the working class, minorities, or the Third World; assaults on established reputations or the elevation of obscure ones. Afterward, the latitude vouchsafed these special subjects was extended wherever ideas claimed a hearing on the basis of their author's generous concern for humanity. Eventually it became accepted that a writer's speculations and prejudices, rather than being subject to skepticism on account of their subjectivity, should be honored for their intentions. The war against the intellect had brought about a decline of discourse—a slackening in the process of critical evaluation.

With traditional constraints on discourse suspendable, the way

was open in the course of the 1970s and 1980s for untrammeled expression of the oppositionist ideology that had fueled the original
assault on values in the 1960s. This ideology in fact grew into an accepted orthodoxy. Guilt and recrimination toward history, culture,
government, and institutions became accepted scholarly attitudes. In
the typical manner of orthodoxies, these attitudes ceased being put
forth as arguments: they had become unstated assumptions, grown
so familiar as hardly to merit comment. The result was that, whether
out of fear or dulled perceptions, reviewers whose business it was to
define and evaluate the arguments that came before them no longer
so much as mentioned, let alone challenged, the new orthodoxies. In
the universities especially, an atmosphere of intimidation came to
prevail. Those who continued to uphold the standards of objectivity
were regarded as insensitive and reactionary. Eventually there took
place an institutionalization of resistance to authority of all kinds.
Literary critics rejected traditional interpretations, scholars found
the formal limitations of their disciplines stifling, and humanists objected to the established canon of great works.

A striking symptom of the new state of mind was the dramatic
valedictory to the historical profession made in 1971 by the historian
Martin Duberman. Accusing himself of wasting ten years as a conventional, uninspired academic biographer, he vowed in future to
avoid the disciplined, scholarly approach. In its place he proposed to
employ an unspecified psychological subjectivism—to depend, as far
as one could make out, on hunches rather than conventional historical explanation. The latter presumably rested on a cold, rigid formal-
ity for which genuine feeling would be substituted. But Duberman's
illustration of the difference between the two was hardly convincing.
As I wrote at the time:

> In his book on Charles Francis Adams, Duberman recalls, "I
> had little difficulty describing why he decided to become a law-
> yer." Now [i.e., in 1971] he suspects that it may not have been
> the "prestige and income" of the law that influenced his subject
> but rather "the hope of duplicating the achievements of his fa-
> ther, John Quincy Adams," tempered by a "fear that he would
> not measure up to his father." The new speculation reflects Du-
> berman's new interest in the impalpables of psychology, which,
> he implies, the canons of scholarship prevented him from em-

ploying. In fact, his original explanation was *un*-historical, since the attractions of money and prestige always may be motives for going into the law. The new explanation, on the other hand, could easily have been arrived at within the traditional discipline of history, and indeed has been arrived at by traditional scholarship.

Given the palpable inadequacy of the case against traditional intellectual standards, the silence of most scholars and intellectuals in the face of the war against the intellect stands out as a phenomenon of equal interest and importance to the war itself. At Stony Brook, for example, the importance of the faculty meeting I attended had to do not so much with the campus radicals and their aims as with the acquiescent majority. It was their willingness to suspend critical judgment that would have the most lasting consequences. That they were seized by strong feelings is not to be denied. But another element had come into play as well—one that was made clear in a report on the Yale meeting from which the Panther resolutions derived.

Writing in the *New Republic* shortly after that meeting, the Yale Law School professor Alexander Bickel described the circumstances surrounding it. On their way to deliberate, the faculty members had passed along a gauntlet of students. The students' intimidating presence, Bickel reported, strongly influenced the conduct of the meeting and the vote in favor of the Black Panther resolutions. At Stony Brook, as it happened, the students were actually allowed in the lecture hall where the meeting convened. The faculty's first act was to approve their unprecedented attendance: seated on the lecture stage and in the balconies overlooking—and overseeing—the proceedings. Intimidation had become respectable. Henceforward it would prove to be one of the driving forces of the war against the intellect.

The essays in this volume trace such developments as the acceptance of intellectual intimidation and the turn to subjectivisim in discourse from the mid-1970s to the mid-1980s. Each essay was conceived as a case study examining an episode in the war against the intellect. In reflection of my interests and expertise, four fronts of that war are dealt with—two of them literary, one historical, and one general. A more systematic survey could be conducted showing the outcome of the war against the intellect in other fields. But I have preferred to look closely at a few representative cases, hoping to evoke through them, and through this introduction, a sense of the larger picture.

The first section, "The American Heritage," opens with an early episode of antirationalism: an attack on scholarly editing for its putatively heartless similarity to American technological warfare in Vietnam. The essay on this attack, "The American Heritage and Its Guardians," shows that the scholars subjected to it had long hidden behind a badly flawed façade of objectivity. In this as in later episodes, then, the guardians of culture prove to have rendered themselves vulnerable to attack well before the onset of the war against the intellect. (A later essay, "Civilization's Malcontents: Responses to *Typee*," touches on scholarly editing again to show how within a few years the scholars had internalized the accusations against them, compromising their principles in their desire to be part of the new sensibility.) "Ezra Pound on American History" is a detailed exposé of scholarship on Pound. But the cultural point again lies with the response of the literary-critical community: one having to do this time with a willingness to tolerate the self-serving obfuscations of the Poundians. Thanks to the war on the intellect, special-interest groups—here a poet's cult following; elsewhere women, blacks, homosexuals, Chicanos—had come to be regarded as immune from ordinary standards.

The section "Literary Criticism" opens with "The Decline of Criticism," an essay on some early manifestations of the assault on objectivity and literary values now commonly denoted by the term *deconstruction*. Once again it emerges that academics had themselves prepared the intellectual soil—starting as far back as the 1950s—for an attack on literary values. The related essay, "The Politics of Deconstruction," cites the deconstructionists' own statements of political intention in order to draw out some implications of the deconstructive habit of mind for other disciplines. Finally, "Feminist Literary Criticism" shows that like some male academics before them, feminist critics have abandoned traditional canons of valuation. The consequences are shown to be deleterious at once to their movement and to those who, as with deconstruction, shrink from the defense of literary values.

The section "American Literature" has to do with the wide acceptance by academics in this field of countercultural, anti-Western, and even anti-American views. "Literary Scholarship and Disparaging

American Culture" examines several books on American literature containing such views, which go unchallenged by the rest of the profession. "Civilization's Malcontents: Responses to *Typee*" concentrates on the denigration of Western civilization. In order to satisfy this imperative of the war against the intellect, critics of *Typee* have been forced into grotesque exaggerations and misreadings—again allowed to go unremarked and unchallenged by their complacent colleagues.

The section "The Decline of Standards" explores some results of the war against the intellect. "Plagiarism and the Literary Conscience" finds a widespread refusal to enforce what might be described as the most elementary standard of civilized discourse: that it not be dishonest. "The Demotion of Man" discusses the final stage of the war against the intellect: a widespread compulsion to denigrate Western civilization and its works as seen in history, anthropology, and popular culture. "The Dark Age of the Humanities" argues that the rejection of Western values has proceeded furthest in humanities education. Taking up the same problem dealt with in *The Closing of the American Mind* by Allan Bloom, the essay offers a less hopeful defense of the humanities than his. The epilogue, "The Academic Assault on Allan Bloom," printed here for the first time, deals with the demagogic response by academics to Bloom's critique of the university. Their rejection of his account of intellectual decline (one that runs parallel to my own) was conducted in a manner so invidious that the academic critics managed to go a long way toward confirming his case against them.

Taken together, my essays trace the war against the intellect from late 1960s incursions of countercultural attitudes such as antitechnology and the patronizing of special-interest groups, to an escalated attack on America and Western values. The theme that emerges is the steady evolution of the Vietnam-period call to suspend reason in favor of political goals to an assault, by the 1980s, on reason itself. But the beginnings of the war against the intellect to go back further than the Vietnam War. As early as 1961 dissatisfaction with the Cold War had begun to undermine the status of reason and objectivity. A scholarly review by the Harvard historian Oscar Handlin of William Appleman Williams's *Contours of American History* may well mark the point at which the issue was drawn.

Handlin found in the book under review a misuse of historical evidence so egregious as to render its Cold War revisionist thesis quite beneath serious consideration. Astonishingly, though, despite Handlin's stature his seemingly definitive dismissal was itself dismissed by his professional colleagues. For them the originality of a thesis outweighed the traditional requirement that it be buttressed by evidence. For his part, William Appleman Williams defended the manipulation of evidence questioned by Handlin as a technique of "seriatim quotations," a kind of imaginative approach similar to that of the literary critic. Here was a challenge to the very basis of history's claim to be regarded as a discipline: its objective criteria for evaluating evidence. Yet historians who commented on the matter treated it as a question of manners in which they found Handlin's strenuous disapproval more deserving of censure than William Appleman Williams's misuses of evidence.

This response of the professionals, once again, was of far greater importance than the actions of those who were undermining scholarship. The professionals no doubt trusted that Cold War revisionism and the doctrine of seriatim quotations would simply go away, and in this they were right. The consequences of their having tolerated these theories, however, proved to be far more extensive than they could have imagined. In the first place, Cold War revisionism gained a kind of respectability by default in spite of its demise as a viable theory. In the second place, as Handlin exhaustively demonstrated in his *Truth in History* in 1975, from 1961 onward the status of historical evidence continued to be undermined to the point where virtually any radical theory was able to gain a hearing. At the same time, it can be added, similar challenges to objectivity were mounted in other intellectual areas with similar results.

In 1963, for example, Norman O. Brown captivated many otherwise astute critics with a so-called psychoanalytic interpretation of history in his *Life against Death*. Brown claimed to be applying Freud's theory of sublimation to history; actually he altered the theory to suit his purposes as he went along. In a notable but neglected exception to the praise lavished on *Life against Death*, Lionel Abel called Brown's theorizing "important nonsense." Abel demonstrated that "there is no intelligible notion of sublimation in Brown's discussion" and showed that Brown consistently abused the conventions for quoting authorities so as to confuse the distinction between what they had said and his own argument.

It was not long afterward that Harold Bloom, claiming to employ Freud's related theory of repression, declared his explicit intention purposely to misread Freud and other authorities. This time there were some who demurred. Charles Altieri, for example, found in Bloom "an incredible sloppiness and arrogance towards logic and discursive reasoning which makes me wonder how literary criticism maintains even the minimum level of respectability it has among intellectual disciplines." But at the time Altieri wrote—the late 1960s—the war on the intellect had proceeded to the point where Bloom's step of separating theories from evidence was no longer shocking. Accordingly, Bloom's reputation never suffered from such few aspersions on his method as were made. And eventually an admiring book was written on him in which his willful misrepresentations of Freud along with his "usual audacious and dubious blurring of distinctions" could be regarded as positive accomplishments.

In the same year as *Life against Death,* Lionel Abel again observed, rationality came under a different kind of attack in the Broadway production of Peter Weiss's play *Marat/Sade.* At the climax of the performance of this play, the inmates of the insane asylum that has held the Marquis de Sade during the French Revolution break out and cavort madly about the stage. During this scene, Abel reported, "there was an unmistakable feeling of solidarity with them on the part of the audience." This feeling was soon to become familiar in the counterculture's mix of frenzy and revolutionary élan. Abel regarded the audience's attitude as exhibiting both bad taste and a taste for nihilism, but noted that these were symptoms that could not be argued with.

It appears in retrospect that there emerged during the early 1960s a dissatisfaction and weariness with reason itself. It was probably no accident that the first challenge to objective scholarship to be widely tolerated was that of Cold War revisionism, since the weariness seems to have been a product of the long East-West struggle. Scholars felt much as did theatergoers, and each relieved their feelings through their own kinds of repudiation of strict rationality. Then in the late 1960s, after nearly five years of the war in Vietnam, the war against the intellect intensified. The year 1968 saw challenges to settled attitudes of every kind. In the context of anti-Vietnam War sentiment, Noam Chomsky spoke for many intellectuals when, as I wrote at the time, he began to regard it as "a desecration and an insult to the Vietnamese people for him coolly to go on discussing the issues of the war." Activism had to replace intellect, it came to be widely felt; at the very least, intellect had to be put at the service of activism—at whatever cost to intellect.

I discussed this point of view in a review of books on the Vietnam War by Mary McCarthy and Susan Sontag. Both authors, I reported, had "begun to doubt the efficacy and place of reason at the present moment in history." The books under review were surprisingly explicit. At the end of *Hanoi,* for example, Mary McCarthy revealed having come to feel that "those virtues as a person and a writer which she had always cultivated and prided herself upon—fair-mindedness, disinterestedness, objectivity—had come to seem to her like mere 'fossil remains.' In face of the exigencies of the Vietnamese, 'the license to criticize was just another capitalist luxury, a waste product of the system.'" Susan Sontag showed herself more aware than McCarthy of how damaging such an attitude could be for an intellectual. Yet, although "some of what I've written evokes the very cliché of the Western left-wing intellectual idealizing an agrarian revolution," she wrote, she was persuaded of the rightness of using "some elements of Marxist or neo-Marxist language again," and concluded that it was worth putting objectivity aside since she had found "North Vietnam to be a place which, in many respects, *deserves* to be idealized."

These sentiments have since been recognized as epitomes of a particular response to the Vietnam experience. What has been little recognized—and least of all by the guardians of culture—has been their persistence in other forms through the 1970s and 1980s. Each of my essays argues that during these years the terms of discourse were altered to the detriment of objectivity and the spirit of disinterestedness. The essays also argue that those who have been put under assault in the war against the intellect, though faced with fundamental challenges to everything they stand for, have persisted in reacting as if to minor disagreements or points of etiquette. When challenged directly, they typically minimize the importance of the issues. Then, after the particular incident into which they were drawn has been resolved, even though they may have nominally stood on the side of objectivity and standards, they prove to have imbibed some portion of the relativist or subjectivist assumptions that were put forward.

Intellectual unconsciousness such as this, it has seemed to me, requires first of all that the stakes involved in each particular episode be unequivocally defined. Only secondarily do my essays speculate on the reasons for the disappointing record of the intellectuals. Any further inquiry into these reasons would have to take into account the role of careerism in securing either silence or acquiescence from those under attack. Oscar Handlin mentions the natural timidity of academics as a factor, and others have noted that the pressure to publish has lured many into some of the new, easily mastered pseudo-disciplines. Insofar as my own essays mention acquiescence, they tend to emphasize the tremendous sway exerted over intellectuals by challenges to authority. All original thought, after all, constitutes such a challenge, which no one in the intellectual community wishes to stifle. It can be but a short step from concern for the nurturance of new ideas to an unthinking toleration of faulty methods. I also call attention several times to the power of intimidation referred to earlier in this introduction. The physical confrontations of the student revolts were not forgotten after the 1960s—either by professors and intellectuals or by those who went on to challenge them in other areas.

Throughout the war against the intellect a few scholar-intellectuals have resisted incursions into their fields, and my essays are often indebted to them. Notable in addition to writings mentioned in this introduction has been the work in literature of Helen Gardner (*In Defense of the Imagination*) and René Wellek (*The Attack on Literature*), in American studies of Kenneth Lynn (*The Air-Line to Seattle*) and James Tuttleton, and in history of Jacques Barzun (*Clio and the Doctors*), J. H. Hexter (*On Historians*), and Gertrude Himmelfarb (*The New History and the Old*). My contribution to the efforts of these writers has been to call attention to how widely and in what guises the decline of discourse has spread, to point out the role played by ideology in the process, and to criticize those who have remained silent. Above all else, the essays in *The War against the Intellect* challenge scholars and intellectuals to reaffirm the standards of discourse, and to rise to their defense no matter under what aegis they are put in peril.

THE
AMERICAN
HERITAGE

THE AMERICAN
HERITAGE
AND ITS
GUARDIANS

IN RECENT YEARS the idea of what constitutes history has been extended to include oral traditions, physical objects, village and church records, and even gravestone inscriptions. Yet for the most part the written record, historical and literary, remains the major depository of the national heritage. Since 1960 several editing projects have attempted to arrange the written record of America into a modern, scholarly format. Historical scholars have reissued the papers of early American statesmen, and literary scholars the works of nineteenth-century American writers. Like Gothic cathedrals built over hundreds of years, the projects themselves have become institutions; and like other institutions, they have been attacked and defended, seen individual contributors come and go, and evolved in their purposes. The several hundred volumes that have appeared, and the several hundred that have not yet appeared, raise a number of questions about the uses of a nation's heritage.

During the present century, students of post-classical literature and of history began to appreciate the value of authentic texts. They learned that nineteenth-century editions of journals and letters by the famous not only were incomplete, but often had passages rewritten by descendants anxious to cover over what appeared to them as imperfections of character and excesses of expression. Henry Adams once asked a historian if he could confirm that John Adams, Henry's

3

great-grandfather, had called Alexander Hamilton "a bastard brat of a Scotch peddler." He had, but Henry's father had left the phrase out of his edition of John Adams's writings. Even literary works, it developed, were affected by the taste and sometimes by the blue-penciling of editors, friends, and wives. Mark Twain's wife and his friend William Dean Howells prevailed on him to soften and make less colloquial some of Huckleberry Finn's language; Nathaniel Hawthorne's wife rewrote his journals for publication; and editors reworked Emily Dickinson's poems to make them scan and rhyme according to prevailing ideas of poetic correctness.

In the cases where tendentious editing did not take place, less obvious changes of punctuation, spelling, and capitalization diluted the flavor of old works, and sometimes disguised their meanings. When an eighteenth-century statesman calls a man "Ambitious," his capitalization calls attention to a theory of behavior that implies much more than the desire to get ahead. An edited rendering of this judgment, with a lowercase "ambitious," could leave a historian partly ignorant of the political behavior he was trying to analyze. He might not recognize that the man believed to be infected with Ambition could inspire distrust all his life. Even in the absence of significant editorial alterations, the cumulative effect of modernizing or "normalizing" old texts misrepresents them to some degree. On the other hand, the sincerest effort to recover the true flavor of a faded manuscript also may end in misrepresentation. What is one to print when the writer sometimes makes the "a" in "ambition" halfway in size between a capital and lowercase? Leaving aside the details of editorial technique, suffice it to say that it takes time to handle such a problem.

The question of time, it seems to me, is the basis of the controversy that began in 1968 over how the American tradition should be edited. Among reviewers of historical editions, the one objection raised from the beginning had been that too much time was being taken up by exquisite editing and annotation. But the main attack came on the literary side in reviews by Lewis Mumford and Edmund Wilson. Mumford was appalled by an editing scheme for Emerson's journals which reproduced his every revision of manuscript with such fidelity as to make the printed pages literally unreadable. Wilson did not question the texts when he reviewed editions of several novels by Melville and William Dean Howells, but he wrote that the enormous editorial effort expended on them had been a waste of time.

Both reviewers found the volumes at hand bulky, expensive, ugly, and unnecessarily encumbered with editorial essays and tables. Eventually, Wilson's reviews were collected in a pamphlet titled *The Fruits of the MLA* (referring to the Modern Language Association, which sponsors the editions). He and Mumford were answered by several scholars in letters to the editor of the *New York Review of Books,* where their reviews had appeared, and these letters were collected with additions in a pamphlet put out by the MLA titled *Professional Standards and American Editions.*

The scholars argued that they shared their critics' concern for preserving nineteenth-century American literature, but that this end could be accomplished only if they laid the groundwork with their editions. There *were* problems involved in editing these texts, they insisted, but they had solved them unobtrusively by separating their editorial apparatus from the text it accompanied. (The encumbered Emerson edition was explained as a special case, which would be followed by a simplified edition.) Furthermore, their texts were being made available to paperback reprint companies at low cost. If only the editors could be left to their task, they argued, within a few years, perhaps a "decade," they would establish "definitive" editions of American authors. The job would not again need doing in the "foreseeable future." There ended the public debate, without either the technical or the cultural issues being settled.

By coincidence, the relationship of the American government to the American tradition had involved itself in the debate in two ways. Wilson reviewed the American editions because he had lost out to the scholars in bidding for federal support of his rival plan for inexpensive, relatively unedited editions of American works on the plan of the French Pléiade editions. What Wilson saw as a multimillion-dollar boondoggle of the government and the people, the MLA called a significant undertaking that was being subjected to criticisms based on nothing but Wilson's personal disappointment. Lewis Mumford brought in the government in the form of the Vietnam War. His review title, "Emerson behind Barbed Wire," implied a parallel between the lack of humanism evidenced by the editors and the inhumanities of the American military in Vietnam. "The voice in which Emerson calls out to one," he wrote, "is drowned by the whirring of the critical helicopter, hovering over the scene." Wilson and Mumford shared a distrust of technology, which Wilson found operative in the Hinman collating machine used by the editors and Mumford found in the "technological extravagance" of their "automated editing." At the MLA's convention a few months after the Wilson and Mumford reviews, the young antiwar professors who temporarily gained control of the organization adopted this politicized literary terminology. They sold copies of Wilson's *Fruits of the MLA* and offered resolutions calling both for withdrawal from Vietnam and a cutoff of funds for the American editions.

In retrospect, the ruling fashion of the late sixties appears to have been less technology than antitechnology, along with a rhetorical confusing of unrelated issues with the Vietnam War. Wilson's and Mumford's attacks set the tone for easy dismissal of the American editions by most of the English profession. Yet there is nothing intrinsically antihumanistic in collating textual variants, or in employing a machine to simplify that task. Poking fun at the Hinman collator has a gentry-like ring of favoring handcraftsmanship at the expense of the worker. In their contempt for what Mumford called the "technological extravagance and human destitution" of the editors, critics unhumanistically continue to treat them as if they were machinelike. In fact, they have proved to be fallible men bemused by an apparently scientific method.

Since 1968 the debate over editing has become yet more technical in its terminology, and consequently has faded from public view. The very journals that continue the discussion are probably unknown to most professors of literature and history, not to speak of readers of the *New York Review of Books*. The titles of these journals might almost be imagined to support Wilson's and Mumford's recoil from dry professionalism: *Bulletin of the Bibliographic Society of America, Editing Nineteenth Century Texts, Jahrbuch für Amerikanstudien, Library, Modern Philology, Proof, Serif, Studies in Bibliography*. But the new debate has favored the assumptions of neither side of the old. And rather than resolving the issue of how to edit a written tradition, it has raised the questions of who will use the tradition and how its guardians should manage it.

Where Edmund Wilson questioned the need for editorial scholarship and above all its slowness, some editorial scholars have taken to questioning the method itself. Professor Fredson Bowers of the University of Virginia had introduced an editorial technique developed in connection with Renaissance plays. There, sloppy compositors worked from faulty manuscripts that in many cases probably came not from the author but from actors' copies. The modern editor was faced with widely differing printed versions, no one of which could be regarded as more correct than any other. W. W. Greg and others evolved a method whereby the best from each version could be utilized. Greg identified and used as his basic text the earliest printed version, which he called his "copy-text." Then he compared this with later versions to see if he could detect an author's hand in the variations that arose. Where he could do so he incorporated the changes, leaving aside variations accountable as printer's errors or normalizings. The resultant text was "eclectic," since it coincided with no previously printed version. Being the result of a tested theory, though, it carried more authority than an editor's choice of the best version of each line.

The theory was simple. One would hardly recognize Greg's formulation of it as a major contribution without knowing that when he published "The Rationale of Copy-Text" in 1949, more than fifty years of editing Renaissance plays had gone by without anyone's having codified a statement of principles. The earliest edition of a work, Greg explained, should be taken as "copy-text" by the modern editor even in cases where an author revised later editions, because the first edition remains the closest to his manuscript. When an author corrects and revises later editions, he concerns himself with his *words*—those the printer has got wrong and those he sees a chance to improve. In this concern with words, an author tends not to pay attention to printers' errors of spelling and punctuation. These elements are called "accidentals" by modern textual scholars, while (in keeping with our age's need for jargon) words are called "substantives." If one selected the *last* edition as copy-text, one would have the author's latest corrections but not the spelling and punctuation with which he had begun. By starting with the earliest edition and incorporating only changes in the words, one ends with the closest possible approximation of the author's intention. The theory, Greg emphasized, was only a guide. One had to rely on judgment in determining which changes were authorial, and one had to be prepared to depart from theory when circumstances required. It might be evident, for example, that the author *had* paid attention to some of his "accidentals"; in this case the editor would be forced to breach the theory in following the revisions. Throughout, of course, the editor had to distinguish between errors that he *should* correct and words, spellings, and punctuations that he didn't like but should let stand as having more authority than his personal taste or his hunch that an awkward expression wasn't really what his author intended.

Had Wilson and Mumford looked into the theory of copy-text they would have realized that Fredson Bowers employed a method with as much dependence on taste and judgment as any other scholarly activity. Had they looked into the backgrounds of the other editors using the Greg technique, they would have discovered that most of them had backgrounds in literary but not textual scholarship. Instead of a monolithic technocracy, they represented a group of neophytes learning as they went along. Their critics missed not only the really serious mistakes that resulted, but the causes of those mistakes as well.

In 1964 the Center for Editions of American Authors came into existence with federal money denied to Edmund Wilson for his Pléiade-like edition. It took under its wing some editions already in progress and initiated and approved others during the next few years. It awarded a seal for the title pages of volumes that met its editing requirements. The editions bearing this seal comprise the American Editions. They include Stephen Crane, John Dewey, Ralph Waldo Emerson, Nathaniel Hawthorne, William Dean Howells, Washington Irving, Herman Melville, William Gilmore Simms, Henry David Thoreau, and Mark Twain. (Other projects, like the writings of Walt Whitman, have received partial approval and funds from the center.) The statement of editorial method by Fredson Bowers for his edition of Hawthorne in effect became the center's standard, as that edition became its model.

In 1950 Julian P. Boyd issued the first volume of the *Writings* of Thomas Jefferson. In the same year the Federal Records Act empowered the National Historical Publications Commission to support additional projects. Boyd's statement of editorial method became the guide for the editions of statesmen's papers that soon followed. These included the writings of John Adams and the Adams family, Benjamin Franklin, Alexander Hamilton, John Jay, James Madison, and George Washington. Boyd, with a minimum of theorizing, dedicated himself to collecting variant forms of documents, selecting the best, and transcribing faithfully but not quite literally. Without correcting texts or changing spelling, he expanded contractions, eliminated eccentric punctuation, and within brackets supplied missing words and parts of words. As an example of his method, Boyd offered a sentence by Jefferson (first rendered literally and then in its edited form):

> Carleton havg hrd yt we were returning with considble re-infmt, so terrifd, yt wd hve retird immedly hd h. no bn infmd by spies of deplorble condn to wch sm pox had redd us.

> Carleton having heard that we were returning with considerable reinforcement, [was] so terrified, that [he] would have retired immediately had he not been informed by spies of [the] deplorable conditions to which smallpox had reduced us.

In responding to its critics, the Center for Editions of American Authors stressed "the permanence" of its editions. Bowers explained that these were "definitive" texts, "the ultimate form that need never be done again." In 1972 he ended a defense by writing of the editions, "The results will live—we guarantee you—and will still be a source of pride to our great great great grandchildren." In the meantime, a new kind of reviewer of the editions appeared: scholarly, precise, trained in the same school as Bowers, and more devastatingly critical than the humanists. Several of these critics questioned the applicability of copy-text theory to nineteenth-century American works. Fredson Bowers, they charged, was unfamiliar with the period, as evidenced by his ignorance of distinctive American spellings. In reviewing Bower's edition of Hawthorne's *The Marble Faun,* John R. Freehafer concluded that 250 editorial emendations, many of them spellings, were incorrect. Elsewhere, assessing all of Bower's Hawthorne volumes, he concluded: "The vast majority of the . . . emendations in these texts can already be identified as mistaken." In response, some of the editors retreated. One explained that the center's seal of approval merely stated that a given book was "*An* Approved Text," not that it claimed to be the only or definitive edition. Another admitted that the American Editions were "far from perfect," and a third referred to editorial "boondoggling," "delay," and "incompetence." Coming full circle from the original claims of perfection, this editor concluded, "No one is qualified to say that all the editions will not have to be redone."

In contrast, the writings of the statesmen have been received with gratitude and awe. Their interpretive notes may be said to constitute a new school of historical scholarship. Boyd and Lyman H. Butterfield of the Adams Papers have gone furthest in raising and answering historical questions in their annotations. Comparing their approach with the minimum of notation in other historical editions, some reviewers have found it "excessive" and obtrusive. Such criticism has been confined to a few passing remarks, though; no one has offered systematic criticism, and most of those who have raised any question have concluded that if Boyd, Butterfield, and their assistants can sustain their brilliance, then their results bar complaints that rest on theoretical grounds. Indeed, the only edition that may prove less than satisfactory, the Hamilton *Papers,* has erred in the direction of editorial restraint. One volume, adhering strictly to the decision to print all that Hamilton wrote, contains little more than his transcriptions from Madison's diary and his notes for the *Federalist* papers. (Judging the matter from a literary perspective, however, I would guess that when critics compare the *Federalist* notes with the final versions, they may find them more valuable than the reviewer in the *William and Mary Quarterly* suspected.) Two other Hamilton volumes print without comment documents that raised editorial questions for Julian P. Boyd. Boyd's solutions resulted in the spectacular discovery that Hamilton had treasonously meddled in American foreign policy. (Boyd published his analysis in 1964 in *Number 7: Alexander Hamilton's Secret Attempts to Control American Foreign Policy, with Supporting Documents.*)

Putting aside exceptional achievements, the historical editors still unquestionably have had far greater success than their literary counterparts. The explanation appears to lie in one crucial editorial decision on which the two groups differ. Where the literary editors opt for an eclectic text, the historians opt for faithful transcription of a single text, with the variants indicated in footnotes. With an eclectic text, the problem of variants is solved at the expense of making them disappear from view; with the texts given by the historical editors, the reader can estimate the importance of the variants (with the help of suggested interpretations in the footnotes). Only the editors of the Hamilton *Papers,* again, appear to have gone wrong here, and then not theoretically but practically. They reprint the earliest versions of Hamilton's newspaper articles—a choice with a superficial resemblance to the copy-text approach—even when other versions are more complete and more desirable. The case does not suggest that historical editors should adopt the method of eclectic text; nevertheless, one has the feeling that each set of editors might usefully have advised the other. For the historical editor requires a literary appreciation of nuance, while the literary editor needs the historian's respect for fact. (Significantly, perhaps, the most successful editor, besides Boyd, was a literary scholar doing a historical edition: Lyman H. Butterfield.) The two sets of editors, with their opposite kinds of problems, recall Shakespeare's tragedies in which each hero is faced with the one problem he cannot handle. If only Iago had tried to trick Hamlet instead of Othello, and if only Othello instead of Hamlet had been given the task of avenging his father! With the literary editions, the editors' tragic flaw was respect for language.

In explaining his enormous effort to record the slight differences among variant manuscripts and texts, Fredson Bowers points out that an accumulation of small changes by proofreaders and compositors can affect the "texture" of a work, with an ultimate effect on meaning. He attempts to winnow out these changes in order to reconstruct the author's work in its original state. But mark how good intentions may bring more harm than bad. It would be unfair to the author literally to transcribe his manuscript without correcting his obvious oversights. If he went through the manuscript changing a character's name, for example, but forgot to make the substitution in one instance, the editor must supply the deficiency. (A historical editor, in the parallel instance of his author's writing a name incorrectly, prints the wrong name followed by a bracketed correction.) An eclectic text, therefore, becomes an attempt not only to eliminate unauthorized changes made in previous editions, but to recapture "the author's intention." This phrase, which appears in the title of a Center for Editions of American Authors booklet, opened the door to chaos. For did not the author intend that his misspellings be corrected? And did he not further intend that his variant spellings be regularized, along with his capitalization and hyphenation and punctuation? Interpreted liberally, as it has been, the method of attempting to plumb the author's intention can mean more, rather than less, tampering with his text.

But these liberalities were only the beginning. What if the author's intentions changed? Bowers, following Greg, aimed to discover the author's *final* intentions, but this soon proved inadvisable in numerous situations. The editors of Melville's *Typee* decided to reject many of Melville's own revisions made when he went over the first, English edition of his novel to prepare it for publication in America. They concluded that "original intentions may often be more valid than final intentions." In their judgment, Melville's publisher may have pressured him to alter certain expressions that the publisher feared unacceptable to American readers. Along with these changes, they rejected Melville's apparent attempts to counter criticisms of his narrator by reviewers of the English edition. The reviewers had found the narrator's speech too literary for an ordinary seaman, and in response Melville apparently tried at several points to make him sound more salty. The editors judged these changes out of keeping with the book's original texture. In all, the editors developed six categories of changes by Melville that they could reject for violating his original intentions, or his "true" intentions, or his "concept of the book as an artistic whole." The last and least category, fittingly, contains the flaw in their logic.

According to the concept of an artistic whole, revisions of *any* type made by Melville could be rejected when these revealed the influence of later developments in his style. This was to introduce, in the name of scholarly objectivity, an essentially subjective basis for editorial revisions. Far from being technocrats icily determining accurate texts with the help of machines, the editors were awash in a sea of speculation. The final product of their guesses, "authorized" by the Center for Editions of American Authors, would not have been authorized by Melville, by either his English or American publisher, or by anyone else connected with his book in the nineteenth century. The meddlers among Melville's contemporaries, while they were ready enough to make changes of their own, at least restricted themselves to a single concern. In contrast, the modern editor revises in several ways. He rewrites usage, punctuation, spelling, capitalization, and hyphenation—sometimes supplying a correction and sometimes retaining an incorrect form even when the author has changed it. For example, in *Typee* a changed possessive, though evidently Melville's correction, is rejected because by copy-text theory an author pays no attention to "accidentals."

Thus has the greatest respect for language, together with copy-text theory, resulted in versions of Melville and others that should be called almost anything but "definitive." Furthermore, the same concern for language has ended in undermining the originating premise of modern textual scholarship: rescue of the text from bowdlerizers, censors, and correctors.

Possibly the most stunning liberty with an author's text in the twentieth century occurs in a 1962 edition of *Billy Budd,* completed just before the American Editions began. In setting the execution of Billy Budd in historical context, Melville recalls the similar executions, aboard the American navy ship *Somers,* of "a midshipman and two petty officers." The editors' note 281 reads:

> Philip Spencer was an acting midshipman; Samuel Cromwell "was in fact the boatswain's mate, but the other, Elisha Small, was a plain 'seaman.'" (The present text is emended to read "a midshipman and two sailors.")

Faced with the famous error in Keats's "On First Looking into Chapman's Homer," the same editors presumably would correct it to read:

> . . . like stout Balboa when with eagle eyes
> He stared at the Pacific.

"In fact," their note would read, "it was not Cortez who first reached the west coast of South America."

This is not the place to outline a theory of authorial error. But if simple respect for a writer's own words will not preserve them from editors, Freud's doctrine in *The Psychopathology of Everyday Life* offers the definitive argument against unconsidered editorial corrections. Freud's book made it a matter of common sense that an error usually reveals more than does a controlled statement of intention. The executions Melville referred to in *Billy Budd* took place aboard a ship on which his own cousin had been first lieutenant. Any unconscious exaggeration by Melville of the rank of those executed has possible significance for the astute reader. This is not to say that the error is easily interpreted. Did Melville exaggerate to increase the importance of the parallel with the *Somers*—or out of a vaguely shared guilt over his cousin's complicity in the matter, or both? In any case, for an interpreting age like our own, the change from "petty officers" to "a midshipman and two sailors" is as significant as a nineteenth-century editor's excision of an entire paragraph of sexually explicit or politically dangerous material.*

Historians are prevented from the well-meaning excesses of the American Editions not necessarily by common sense but by their fundamental respect for historical fact. For them both the text and its variants qualify as historical facts. Authors of historical diaries frequently cut passages for revealing too much, rather than for stylistic reasons. Such passages clearly must be preserved. In general, the historian realizes that he cannot know what value a fact may take on for later investigators. He has seen trivia from the traditional point of view—account books, random jottings—become statistics for the newer quantitative historians or data for psychohistorical investigation. As for seemingly insignificant variations among documents, Boyd has demonstrated in his preface to *Number 7* how editorial investigation of these can lead to discoveries.

The literary editors might have learned the same lesson from their editorial predecessors. But they could hardly think of themselves, who worked to *reverse* censorship, as bowdlerizers and censors. Did they not restore the political and sexually offending passages that were changed by Melville, Howells, and Stephen Crane in capitulation to censoring editors? In that restoration process, Fredson Bowers went so far as to remove an important paragraph from Stephen Crane's *Maggie, a Girl of the Streets*. For a second edition three years after the book appeared in 1893, Crane, like Melville, evidently reworked or removed passages that his publisher feared offensive to the genteel. At the same time, naturally enough, he strengthened other passages and removed still others without reference to his editor's requirements. But which were which? Near the end of chapter 17, Crane removed a paragraph describing the prostitute Maggie's lowest point of degradation, her encounter with a "leering," "huge

---

*Some other examples of slips useful to the critic appear in published essays by editors of American Editions. One editor misspells "judgment," while Fredson Bowers writes of "the celebrated English scholar F. L. Leavis" instead of F. R. Leavis. The errors help to reveal a slightly anglicized cast of mind. In the first case, the older but still current English form "judgement" appears; in the other, Leavis evidently has been confused with the older English critic F. L. Lucas. The spellings and errors by American authors that have been corrected by these same editors hold a similar minor interest for the critic.

fat man." Though this was strong stuff, Bowers argued, it was not explicitly sexual; therefore Crane had not removed it in response to editorial pressure. The editor might admire the passage but was bound to cut it in order to honor the author's intention. At this point Bowers might have been expected to notice some theoretical problems.

Who is to say whether in future the results of self-censorship by writers, even though in response to pressure, will not appear at least as characteristic as the versions now being restored? To deny this possibility one has to be convinced that American authors were alienated utterly from the spirit of their age. This was D. H. Lawrence's influential thesis, reflected clearly enough in the editorial supposition that all genteel revisions were unwelcome to their authors. Yet this is simply to apply the cultural values of one age to another. It is, of course, impossible for a scholar entirely to avoid error. He invites it, though, when he turns a cultural supposition into a tool of analysis by assuming that revisions concerning sexual and political matters must have been made against the author's wishes. The editorial revisions made on this theory, reflecting the politically and sexually progressive 1960s and 1970s, stand a good chance of one day looking as much like censorship as the most notorious nineteenth-century bowdlerizations.

All this is avoided by a historical approach. But such is the lack of concern for history in the American Editions that an editor defending Bowers's silent corrections of Hawthorne's accidentals can write, "Students of the history of punctuation and spelling will regret this loss [as will students of the development of Hawthorne's style, it may be added], but most users, it seems to me, will ordinarily find the arrangement a sensible compromise." The editors have come a long way from their original proud boasts of professionalism to this genial defense of sloppiness. Partly they have retreated in the face of critics, but in at least equal part they have chosen their own direction. The principles left strewn along the way evidence an abandonment of scholarly principles, even as they trace the rout of literary humanism in our day.

The dismissal of "students of the history of punctuation and spelling" betrays an uneasiness with scholarship that appears elsewhere in recent scholarly editing. Surprisingly, for a project with its reputation for scholarly exhaustiveness, most of the American Editions lack footnotes, bibliography, and indexes. Yet several of the problems arising from variants could have been solved with these and other standard devices utilized in the historical editions. Melville's two petty officers could have been given a note explaining his error; Crane's omitted passage about the fat man could have been included within brackets, in a footnote, or in an appendix. None of these solutions was available because the editors had decided in advance to issue "clear texts," that is, texts entirely free of editorial markings. In the fashion of nonprofit organizations involved in partly commercial projects, they went further in avoiding the appearance of seriousness than a trade publisher would find necessary. (These are days when commercial broadcasters worry about quality while public television producers talk about markets and audience appeal.) As a result, the reader interested in variants among previous versions of a book will find much information hard to find and some omitted altogether.

In retreating from its original claim for "definitive" editions, the Center for Editions of American Authors eventually rested not on its editing but on its editorial apparatus. "A definitive edition," its revised introductory booklet explains, "should never have to be done again, because it presents the evidence." Even if the editing should prove less than perfect, in other words, each volume retains permanence by recording in its scholarly appendixes all the variants that would be required for revisions, in the unlikely event that these should prove necessary. As another of the center's booklets emphasizes, "There can be no silent emendations." But this alternate claim to definitiveness will not stand either. In the William Dean Howells edition, "obviously needed punctuation" is "silently" supplied, though no one has estimated how extensively. However, one center editor estimates that Bowers's *House of the Seven Gables* contains "three or four thousand" unrecorded emendations. (It was this loss of the *record*, not of Hawthorne's actual spelling, that the reviewer thought the student of spelling and punctuation might regret.) In addition, in the case of Bowers's *The Marble Faun*, "A reader in search of a key item of information may look in thirteen places without finding it; or he may find that it is the subject of several notes or discussions, all of them incomplete."

Some of these shortcomings may be traced to a second important decision: to omit explanatory notes. At the very least, this has prevented any of the exploratory scholarship that distinguishes the historical editions. In addition, in the opinion of one critic, a number of incorrect emendations stemming from an unfamiliarity with certain nineteenth-century expressions could have been avoided in the process of gathering information for explanatory notes. The absence of scholarship, in short, has resulted in books that satisfy neither the scholar, who finds too little editorial apparatus, nor the general reader, who finds too much.

As a further result of these procedures, instead of having completed editorial work on American books "for all time," as Bowers thought, the center's editors have in fact laid an additional task on the future: that of combing their editions for silent emendations and errors. Anyone preparing an edition in the future would first have to check the center's texts against previous editions and against manuscripts where they are available. This is because all emendations have not been listed, and because of what a recent favorable reviewer of several Mark Twain volumes described as "a few mistypings that escaped even the standards set by the Center." The new editor then would have to compare successive printings of each center text; for the second impression of *The Scarlet Letter*, at least, "has been revised without notice." He would have to avoid relying on Bowers's statement of editorial principles, since the various series differ from one another in their methods. For example, where the Hawthorne and Melville volumes restore passages removed by the author in his apparent response to censorship, the William Dean Howells edition honors authorial deletions. The Emerson edition does something in between: it accepts authorial additions but rejects "many of Emerson's other late changes." Within the Hawthorne edition itself, different volumes are edited in different ways. *The Scarlet Letter* essentially reproduces the first edition. *The House of the Seven Gables* reproduces Hawthorne's manuscript. *Fanshawe* does neither. Instead it purports to offer a reconstruction of Hawthorne's missing manuscript.

To accomplish this, Bowers studied Hawthorne's spelling and punctuation habits in *The House of the Seven Gables* (except those he had already normalized and modernized). He then postulated which usages in the first edition of *Fanshawe* must have resulted from compositors' corrections of Hawthorne and rejected these in favor of what must have appeared in the missing manuscript. That Hawthorne's style or the styling requirements of his publishers might have changed in the twenty years separating the two books seems not to have occurred to Bowers. Nor does it seem to have occurred to him that Hawthorne, in common with other writers, might have welcomed or at least accepted his publisher's changes, letting them stand when he went over the proof sheets, not because they were accidentals but because he preferred them. But even if Bowers were right in his every supposition about *Fanshawe*, if he achieved with it what he claimed for his version of Stephen Crane's "The Open Boat"—"98 per cent perfection in reprinting what must have been the form and details of the lost manuscript"—the fact would remain that he had produced three different kinds of editions in three volumes of his Hawthorne edition.

These were the absurdities of scholars who distrusted scholarship and who, though they revered language, lacked historical reverence for the word itself. Mumford and Wilson mistook their antagonists when they made them out as crude and opportunistic. Yet in a curious way Wilson and Mumford were right to relate the American Editions to the Vietnam War. It was a period in which one characterized the style of one's opponent, and adopted an alternate style expressing contempt for him. On the one side, humanists, disgusted by the war, found a convenient target in scholars whose methods appeared to resemble the cruel efficiencies of the Pentagon. On the other side, academics opposed to the war frequently confessed past complicity with the military-industrial-university axis way of thinking. Others, more sophisticated, grew defensive about the relevance of their undertaking. Within the English profession, scholarship and new criticism, the two foundations of modern scholarly editing, came under the sharpest attack. Along with others in the profession, the scholarly editors retreated from scholarly values and a staunch championship of the writer's own language. The whirring helicopter hovered over every sensitive person in the intellectual world of the late 1960s, drowning out reasoned discourse and sound scholarship alike.

The editors rightly label as anti-intellectual those attacks on them that simply express opposition to scholarly editing itself. Edmund Wilson weakened his case when he let himself appear to represent the mistaken notion that good taste and good intentions alone are required to edit books. These are not sufficient guarantees of success even when editorial problems do not arise. Leon Edel in his selection of letters by Henry James, for example, admits that his decisions on which letters to include were partly subjective and partly meant to supplement his own biography of James. He then argues that scholars can photocopy the letters he has excluded, but fails to reveal the number and whereabouts of these. Instead of lending support to this sort of high-handedness, Wilson should have pointed to the Pléiade edition of Proust—a corrected, variorum version that is more complete than any other. There is no necessity to regard scholarship and commercial viability as incompatible.

A fine example of their compatibility, in fact, may be found in one of the American Editions, the *Writings* of Thoreau. Here good sense has overcome inappropriate theory. One of the editors, J. Lyndon Shanley, explains that Thoreau's style has *not* been tampered with. "To have regularized the many inconsistencies," he writes, "would have led to misrepresentation of the usage of Thoreau and his time, and would have concealed the fact that usage is always changing." The Thoreau volumes are indexed. And compared to the Hawthorne edition—described by one observer not friendly to Wilson as "a clumsy and pretentious piece of bookmaking"—these are compact and notably easy to read.

One further defense of scholarly editing should be mentioned: in many cases it leads to unexpected discoveries. The American Editions have resulted in new manuscript finds and in new identifications of authorship for a number of minor writings. Some of the historical essays accompanying each volume throw new biographical and critical light by tracing author-publisher relations in previously unpublished letters and unexamined records. These essays are likely to stand as the one significant accomplishment of the editions. However, most of the important errors in nineteenth-century American books were discovered by the 1940s, so the center editors have been able to add but a few footnotes to the history of bibliographical discovery. As for their regularizing, modernizing, and mistaken readings, as well as their typographical errors—the truth is that these have proven disastrous only in terms of failed expectations. For in most cases the texts, though accompanied by introductions, appendixes, and notes, remain essentially the same as in earlier editions.

Recognizing this, Morse Peckham nevertheless has argued that "whether an edition has a high yield or not has nothing to do with whether or not it should have been done." As in a scientific experiment, the fact that a negative has been established should not detract from the respectability of the undertaking. But this argument calls for a distinction between bibliographic scholarship and scholarly editing: the former signifies study, the latter a certain kind of publication. Having bibliographically established the basic reliability of our old editions of American books, the editors need not have reported this discovery in the form of editions priced between fifteen and thirty-five dollars a volume and issued at a collective cost in excess of six million dollars. [As of 1988 the prices ranged up to almost ninety dollars a volume.] For the price of a few periodical articles, we could have learned that *The Scarlet Letter* contains "precisely two independent substantive emendations" and that "both of these turn out to be unnecessary."

A typical product of the 1960s, the American Editions lacked modesty of scale. In seeking the definitive, they failed at being adequate. One thinks of New York State's laughably overpriced Albany Mall; New York City's Lincoln Center, with the echoing acoustics of its Philharmonic Hall; Boston's John Hancock skyscraper, with its glass panels sucked off by the building's self-generated winds; the San Francisco Bay Automated Rapid Transit system, with equipment that failed even when personally attended. Like these other ambitious projects, the American Editions gradually displayed crippling flaws. Unlike the historical editions, most of them are selected, not complete, editions; they include no plans to publish authors' letters, for example. Further, it develops that they have failed at being definitive not only because of errors, but because of the physical impossibility of comparing and recording all the variants as demanded by copy-text theory. Critics have shown that, contrary to editorial claims, the center editors do *not* compare all of the printings of each book. (A "printing" should be distinguished from an "edition." Books often go through four or five editions, each of which can have a half-dozen or more printings.)

As for errors, besides the inevitable ones of judgment and in proofreading, there are fresh errors in the paperback reprints by which the editors justified themselves when responding to Edmund Wilson. Despite elaborate rules for reproducing center texts, for example, one of the few misprints that Bowers could label "significant" is restored to its incorrect nineteenth-century form by the paperback reprint of his text. In the opinion of one reviewer, the American Editions paperbacks have about the same accuracy as the Riverside Hawthorne—the popular nineteenth-century edition they supposedly are displacing. (Since the convenience of scholars is a major argument in favor of the new editions, it should be pointed out that scholars will have the inconvenience of changing their citations from the Riverside Hawthorne so they will refer to Bowers's new edition. Until completion of the new, they will have to cite from both editions, and afterward will still need the Riverside to check the work of fellow scholars who cited from its pages. Thus the arguments are many for sticking to the old edition. As for classroom use, with its explanatory notes and minimal textual emendation, Professor Harry Levin's *Scarlet Letter,* based on the Riverside, is equal to reprints of Bowers's version.)

The whole idea of a project intended to be error-free has an innocently millenarian, American flavor to it, presuming as it does not only that such a thing is possible, but that it is desirable. The opposite cultural assumption appears in the design of French telephones, it has always seemed to me. Expecting that things will go wrong, the French hook an extra earpiece to the side of the instrument, so that when power loss or interference develops this can be held up to the listener's other ear.

The historical editors, though most of them are free of the elaborate perfectionism of the American Editions, have not escaped a touch of the millenarian. Edmund Wilson's complaint about the time that it would take to publish the American Editions applies to the historical ones as well. For Jefferson's *Writings,* Boyd initially projected fifty-two volumes. With eighteen volumes in print, his estimate grew to a hundred. Butterfield began in 1953 with an estimate of over a hundred volumes for his Adams Papers. On retiring in 1975, more than twenty years later, he and his colleagues had issued but twenty volumes. Even if his original estimate were to stand, at least eighty years would be required to complete the edition. The net result of the Adams Papers, and of the other historical and literary projects, comes down to this: the guardians of our tradition have succeeded in keeping it out of print. Fewer of the writings of our eighteenth-century statesmen and nineteenth-century writers are in print today than at the turn of the century.

By the turn of the century or soon after, G. P. Putnam's had published, without subsidy, the writings of Samuel Adams, Franklin,

Hamilton, Jay, Jefferson, Madison, Monroe, Paine, and Washington. The Riverside Hawthorne text was still available, along with collections of James Fenimore Cooper, Emerson, Poe, Mark Twain, Whitman, and, a few years later, Henry James. All the editions had shortcomings, but none so great as the incompleteness of the present editions that have supplanted them. The contrast between the situation then and now suggests that the uses and the users of the nation's heritage have changed. The turn-of-the-century sets were purchased by gentlemen who thought it proper to have such volumes on their shelves. Today's volumes go to libraries for use by scholars. No commercial publisher thinks he can make money by issuing collected editions of American statesmen or writers—not even of Hemingway, Fitzgerald, Dos Passos, Faulkner, or T. S. Eliot.

Very possibly our traditions may be of direct use only to professionals and students, the rest of the population subsisting on historical novels, television dramatizations, and a few images of the past recalled from school days. On the other hand, if editors and publishers begin with this assumption, or something like it, no wider dissemination or deeper understanding of the tradition can be possible. There is no telling who will make use of sets of the American classics if they are made available inexpensively and in readable form. But if they are made only partially available, and if issued for the most part in unwieldly volumes and at great expense, they most certainly will have no general use. Yet the bibliographical scholars have a point when they argue that each time a slightly improved edition is published, the job only has to be done over again soon after it is finished.

I am reminded of a conference on housing in the underdeveloped countries at which Charles Abrams, the city planner, offered as his solution: "Build slums." He was thinking, it would seem, of cities like Brasília which, despite its planners' care to avoid putting up inferior buildings, generated shantytowns that left those planners with the very problem they had set out to avoid. The partial, never-to-be-completed editions of American works are our Brasília, and the occasional paperback reprints and surviving old editions imported from secondhand bookstores are their surrounding shantytowns. Abrams was suggesting, it seems to me, that everyone would be better off in jerry-built houses thrown up quickly and not meant to last more than twenty years. With the population housed, one could afford to let the planners start their utopias. Edmond Wilson's Pléiade, or something like it, should be undertaken for similar purposes. Unlike the planners, the scholars could continue their projects while the cheaper editions were coming out. The scholars could issue limited editions for one another and donate the saved production costs to the slum editions.

Who knows but that the slums might develop some planning ideas for use by the master builders? Hyatt H. Waggoner's one-man edition of *The House of the Seven Gables,* for example, demonstrates how to utilize an author's manuscript without dogmatism or hoopla. Given the typographical errors in the American Editions, it may turn out that a single editor can do better than a team that reads proofs five times, as the present policy dictates. Let us have *all* of Emerson's *Journals,* then, just as he left them. Leave out both his wife's bowdlerizing and the present editors' painstaking reconstruction of his revisions. Who knows? Perhaps this method will turn out to yield a desirable edition. (The most that we are now promised is that, after completing the unreadable Emerson, the same editors will start on a clean text *selection* from it.) Let us have *all* of William Dean Howells, to see how the public likes it. Let us have Walt Whitman's books as he wrote them. No complete *Democratic Vistas* is in print because his editors have chosen to reprint the truncated version Whitman prepared just before his death. Let us have John Adams's writings on government, even though they often contain quotes without quotation marks; otherwise it will take a decade to check all the hidden references for an annotated edition. For such slums as these, many of us will gladly exchange our present dwellings.

The American Scholar, Winter 1975–76

NOTE: None of the projects called for in the last paragraph of this essay has as yet (1988) been carried out. Yet some notable changes have taken place since 1975, when it was written. The Library of America, drawing on both scholarly and previous editions, has undertaken quickly and inexpensively to publish most if not all of the writings of the major American authors, albeit at higher prices than the French Pléiade editions. The Center for Editions of American Authors, somewhat expanded in scope, is now known as the Center for Scholarly Editions. Criticism of the editing practices it oversees continues. Donald Pizer has attacked the editors of Stephen Crane's *The Red Badge of Courage* and Theodore Dreiser's *Sister Carrie,* while Herschel Parker has questioned a variety of editing practices in his *Flawed Texts and Verbal Icons* (1984). In Parker's view, Crane's *Maggie, a Girl of the Streets* as edited by Fredson Bowers—the version adopted by the Library of America—represents "one of the most disheartening mishmashes in textual history."

On the historical side the National Historical Publications Committee has been expanded into the National Historical Publications and Records Commission. A new generation of editors has begun to cut back on the extensive, leisurely footnoting of the Boyd school, and to issue volumes more quickly. As a result, the political writings of John Adams mentioned in the final paragraph have at last begun to appear.

EZRA POUND

ON AMERICAN

HISTORY

THE LONGEST AND MOST ob-
scure section of Ezra Pound's *Cantos* has until recently been all but
ignored. His ten cantos devoted to John Adams, when they are discussed, are described by Poundians as an extreme but viable example
of Pound's poetic method. Old fashioned readers, argue the Poundians, are put off by chronological discontinuities and by apparently
obscure passages, but these fall into place in the harmonious design
of the whole work. This defense at once invokes the authority of
Pound's private terms for modernist poetics—vortex, ideogram,
paideuma—and asserts that he has written nothing but what can be
understood with care by an intelligent general reader. But aside from
such generalizations, since publication of the Adams cantos in 1940
no more than six out of their twenty-five hundred lines have been
explicated, and these incorrectly. The case presents a challenge not
only to the reputations of Pound and his followers, but also to some
of the cherished dogmas of modernism.

The ten Adams cantos (62–71) were published together with ten
so-called Chinese history cantos (52–61). Randall Jarrell, in his 1940
review of the twenty cantos comprising these two groups, declared
that Pound had "deteriorated." "*Cantos* LII–LXXI," he wrote, "contains the dullest and prosiest poetry that he has ever written. These
Cantos are so bad that they would not seem his at all, if they were
not so exactly like the very worst portions of the old ones." Years
later Donald Davie, in his book *Ezra Pound, Poet As Sculptor* (1964),

called the ten Chinese history cantos "pathological and sterile," and added, "The John Adams cantos . . . are composed in the same way as the Chinese History cantos that precede them." Jarrell, however, wrote that Pound showed "a fine feel for anecdotes that carry the quality of a person or an age," and Davie, though disappointed in the results, conceded that Pound was carrying forward his "poetic method." Significantly, neither of these fine poet-critics quoted so much as a line of the Adams cantos, or attempted to convey what he understood or felt about them.

Adams is the subject of Cantos 62 to 71. He is mentioned occasionally in later cantos, notably in 94, and appears in Cantos 31 to 33, which are mostly about Jefferson. In addition, Canto 34 is devoted to John Quincy Adams, his son. Together with Canto 37, on Martin Van Buren, 31–34 and 62–71 are known as the American history cantos. In 62–71 one is faced with eighty pages of unexplained prose quotations. These come from *The Works of John Adams* and include passages from state papers, legal arguments, diplomatic correspondence, and political treatises. The selections have no apparent connection with the rest of the *Cantos*—not even the others on American history. The Adams cantos are not in verse (Jarrell wrote, "The versification of these cantos is interesting: there is none"), though they are printed as poetry. Frequently, it is true, lines are indented, giving a look of poetry to the page. And the most common device also has a poetic look: it is the overrun line in which the latter part of a long sentence spills onto a second line set at the right hand margin.

Comparison with Pound's source, *The Works of John Adams,* reveals that aside from rearrangement on the page, most changes by Pound involve words he has omitted, abbreviated, lengthened, misspelled, misunderstood, or put into slang. Pound's contributions are limited to occasional interpolated phrases, exclamations, and foreign-language tags (the Chinese ideogram for "balance" appears several times, usually following John Adams's mention of either personal restraint or governmental balance of powers). However, many of the Latin tags are from Adams himself. In addition, Pound renders phrases in the ole Ez jargon of his letters. "Says" becomes "sez," "them" becomes "'em," "Dr. Franklin," "Doc Franklin," "soldiers," "sojers," and "navy," pointlessly, "navee." The "Johnnie Adams" of earlier cantos disappears, but Pound having learned that "Chas. H. Adams" is actually Charles *F.* Adams, takes to referring to the editor of the *Works* of John Adams as "Chawles Fwances." For the most part Pound's vulgarizations are identifiable as interpolations: "Philadelphy" and "Baastun," for example, are clearly his own private jokes, endlessly and pointlessly repeated. Frequently, though, there is a misleading appearance of eighteenth-century diction having been reproduced, as in the cases of "Capn Preston" and "Lard Narf" (for Lord North), neither of which appears in the original. Similarly, Pound appears to reproduce the immediacy of old documents when he writes "N. York," "shd," "wd," "recd," or "Mr. A." None of these, though, is abbreviated in the original. When Pound writes, "Mr D (Deane's) recommendations," or "He (Jay) returned yesterday to N. York," he appears to clarify when actually he is obscuring the original. The first line he has copied reads simply, "by Mr. Deane's recommendation" (not "recommendations"), and the second reads, "His Excellency, Governor Jay, returned yesterday to New York."

Pound's own writing, which amounts to a few scattered, single lines in each canto, may be classed as exclamatory interjection. The widely separated phrases of his own in the Adams cantos have the appearance and effect of marginal comments made by a solitary reader for his own satisfaction:

> sojers aiming??
> . . . all bugwash
> Hutchinson sucking up to George IIIrd.
> Damn well right, Mr. Zubly.
> (leaving us no doubt Vergennes was a twister)
> (which seems fairly English)
> (question?)

In the same spirit, when copying a list of names Pound may add one of his own ("KUNG Zoroaster Socrates and Mahomet") or else indicate that he would wish to do so ("add Jay").

In view of their aridity, one can understand the reluctance of a Poundian to look at these cantos in detail. But it is surprising, even in view of their appearance under the protective cloak of modernism, to find that independent critics have treated them with respect for thirty-five years. The Poundians make no distinction between the Pound of the pre-1922 modernist period and the Pound of the *Cantos,* and little distinction between the early cantos and those written during the author's intellectual decline. Pound called the volume in which the Adams cantos appeared "my best book [of poetry]." Accordingly, Poundians are committed to justifying its place in the *Cantos* at large. More surprisingly, critics not ideologically committed to Pound have cooperated in this project. By according a misplaced respectability to a coterie following, they have let themselves be led into acquiescence in partisan accounts of the Adams cantos. In effect this has put them on the side of the claim that the *Cantos* as a whole is a unified work.

Significantly, even the Poundians express reservations about the Adams section before delivering their ritual praise for it—always without specific comment. Daniel Pearlman finds a "general failure of these cantos to achieve poetic intensity." Necessarily, though, in a book subtitled "On the Unity of Ezra Pound's Cantos," he concludes that despite their faults "they do have an orderly structure." In *The Pound Era,* Hugh Kenner, the staunchest defender and only explicator of the Adams cantos, goes so far in the direction of criticism as to call them "ten Cantos of finely culled citations that are bracing but aesthetically dispersive."

In 1975, though, a sourcebook, *John Adams Speaking: Pound's Sources for the Adams Cantos,* by Frederick K. Sanders, rejected the mild reservations of other Poundians. Sanders claimed to present "convincing evidence of the care with which the poet has selected and arranged his materials." Sanders went through the ten volumes of *The Works of John Adams* and located the passages from which Pound quotes; these, keyed by canto and line number, he reprinted in a volume of over five hundred pages.

In a prologue to this volume Carroll Terrell, managing editor of *Paideuma, a Journal Devoted to Ezra Pound Scholarship,* wrote: "'The Adams Cantos' add up to a large vortex just as each of its several parts is a smaller vortex. The stunning result is the image of an Adams dramatically different from the image previously made by analytical historians." Other Poundians have gone so far as to claim that Adams is the hero of the *Cantos.* Yet one searches in vain for a description of the character supposedly drawn by Pound. William Vasse concludes that "it is impossible to give a simple clue to the personality of John Adams. . . . Pound does not attempt a simple explanation in the Adams Cantos, preferring complexity to pat generalization." Clark Emery in *Ideas into Action: A Study of Pound's Cantos* explains, "The character of Adams emerges so clearly from these cantos that they do not need annotation to register an effect." So lucid are they, apparently, that Emery does not find it necessary to make a single comment, offering instead a page of "excerpts selected at random from the Adams cantos." More accurately, though still respectful of the method, Donald Davie writes that "Pound's cuts and compressions and juxtapositions make a nonsensical hurly-burly of Adams' life." Equally unsubstantiated with the claim that Pound discovered a new John Adams is William Vasse's claim that in the Adams cantos and the other American history cantos "by selecting, remodeling, and editing his material . . . Pound recreates from historical documents a new interpretation of American history which is different from that of his sources, and much different from the 'standard' history book."

Pound wrote the American history cantos on Jefferson and John Adams, John Quincy Adams, and Martin Van Buren between 1933 and 1935, and those on John Adams between 1937 and 1939. The latter group coincided with Pound's furthest remove from society, poetry, and humanism. In 1936 he began contributing to the *Fascist Quarterly*. By 1938, when most of the John Adams cantos were being written, Pound was an enthusiastic follower of Sir Oswald Mosely, the English fascist, and of Benito Mussolini. His essays had become a jumble of fascism, anti-Semitism, and the economic theory of Major C. H. Douglas (whose initials Pound originally attached to C. F. Adams). By this time modern criticism had established the practice of separating the author from his work—an additional circumstance to help shield Pound from searching criticism. After all, one could argue, he had continued to write coherent poetry in the 1920s when already under the influence of Major Douglas. Critical theory seemed to dictate that his economic and political ideas, however abhorrent, be kept strictly out of the account.

While the critics were careful to maintain this separation, Pound himself made no attempt to keep his prejudices out of his poetry. His few interpolations among the quoted and paraphrased lines of the Adams cantos—perhaps less than 10 percent of the whole—have largely to do with his personal obsessions. "Schicksal sagt der Führer" (destiny says the Fuehrer), comments Pound after a line which transcribes John Adams's declaration of his trust in providence. And while Pound exhibits no attempt to search out Adams's economic ideas, he emphasizes those that he comes across by means of heavy, black lines or else with anti-Semitic interpolations. In the first Chinese history canto, quotations on money and the Jews falsely attributed to Adams and Franklin ("better keep out the jews") are underscored by five of these lines. In the earlier American history cantos Pound emphasizes unconnected remarks about money by John Quincy Adams and Martin Van Buren, along with their few mentions of the Jews.

Poundian critics have raised questions about the relationship between the early American history cantos and the Adams cantos. Why do those on John Quincy Adams and Martin Van Buren (34 and 37) precede rather than follow the cantos on John Adams, who lived before them? And why does John Adams, who is much less important than Jefferson in 31 to 33, dominate 62 to 71 without reference to his earlier appearance? But these questions, we are told, will trouble only sensibilities trained in old-fashioned, chronologically arranged literature. Such readers are put in their literal-minded places through invocation of the ideogrammatic method, the vortex, or the promised revelation at the end of the *Cantos*. It seems never to occur to the continuing champions of these methods of modernism that their familiar litany is now seventy-five years old and that the sensibility which they present as embattled has been the accepted art language of the century for over fifty years. In any event, no advanced literary conceptions are required to explain the anomalous discontinuity between the John Adams of the early American history cantos and the John Adams of 62 to 71.

Pound, far from arranging and selecting from "historical documents" in the American history cantos, used a single book or set of books for each of them. In 31 to 33 he quoted from letters between Jefferson and Adams appearing in *The Writings of Thomas Jefferson,* in 34 he quoted from a selected edition of John Quincy Adams's diary, and in 37 he used a volume containing Martin Van Buren's autobiography. These cantos were written in the early 1930s. Later Pound wrote that it took him seven years to find a set of John Adams's works in Europe. By 1938 he had that set, and he used it as his single source for Cantos 62 to 71. If John Adams is dwarfed by Jefferson in 31–34, then, it is because Pound is quoting from Jefferson's works, which naturally contain more of Jefferson's letters than Adams's.

Moreover, if Jefferson is forgotten in 62 through 71 it is because he was not prominently before Pound in his source, Adams's works.

Professor Hugh Kenner, the best-known and most influential Poundian, established the terms of criticism for the Adams cantos in his *The Poetry of Ezra Pound* (1951). There he explained that these cantos are "an application to character of the method devised in *Mauberley* for rendering the sensibility of an age. If we read rapidly in search of a narrative we shall be very badly baffled indeed." Noel Stock in *Reading the Cantos* (1967) expresses some reservations about the Adams cantos but assures us: "There is never any doubt where we are, or what we are doing even when we may be ignorant of what Adams is talking about or the situation in which he is involved." Stock, following Kenner, quotes two passages without comment. The fact is that Kenner's commentary on the six lines comprised in these two passages amounts to the only specific explication given to the Adams cantos since their appearance. Kenner wrote as follows:

> When we read in Canto LXII,
>> "Routledge was elegant
>> 'said nothing not hackneyed six months before'
>>> wrote J. A. to his wife,"
> it is less important to know who Routledge was and what he talked about than to apprehend the quality and energy of John Adams' critical mind. Impatience of platitude and exact knowledge of what *was* hackneyed six months before are qualities sufficiently rare in statesmen to justify the chisel-cut effected by these lines.

Now let us see just what kinds of instruction in Adams's character, in American history, and in poetics the Poundians have imbibed from the Adams cantos. Line one: the characterization of Routledge—actually Edward *Rut*ledge—is not by Adams. Line two: "said nothing not hackneyed six months before" does not refer to anything said by Rutledge. Line three: the quoted remark did not appear in a letter by Adams "to his wife." Three lines, three errors.

In the first line Adams is referring to the greatest speech of his career: that delivered on July 2, 1776, in defense of the Declaration of Independence. Self-deprecatingly, he wrote to his friend Samuel Chase that in this speech he had been neither eloquent nor original:

he had merely summarized the six-month-old hackneyed arguments in favor of independence. In contrast, Rutledge of South Carolina was "described by Patrick Henry as the most elegant speaker in the first congress."

How can Pound, and in turn the Poundians, have so garbled this significant but easily grasped moment in American history? Did Pound experience difficulty in interpreting his "historical documents"? Not at all. For he was quoting entirely from volume 1 of the *Works of John Adams,* and this volume consists of a biography of Adams by his grandson, Charles Francis Adams. It is Charles Francis, in fact, who has quoted and "juxtaposed" Patrick Henry's observation on Rutledge with Adams's observation on his own speech in the letter to Chase. Only a man in a frenzy of solipsism could succeed in garbling Charles Francis Adams's straightforward presentation of this comparison. But to bestow on Pound's misquotation the dignity of calling it garbled would be to suggest that an intellectual process was going on where none is detectable. Pound simply copied words from the top of page 230 in the biography for his first line, others from the bottom of 231 for his second, and the mention of a letter from Adams to his wife from the top of the following page. The only detectable principle here is that of quoting from the tops and bottoms of succeeding pages. As for the Poundians, their failure to recognize the context makes it evident that their choice of an historically important quotation was coincidental.

But the confusions go still further. At first it appears that Pound had simply reversed the recipients of the two letters. Instead, he has done something more revealing of his state of mind in the Adams cantos. The last of the three lines quoted by Kenner and the one following it read as follows:

> wrote J. A. to his wife
> I said nothing etc. letter to Chase from John Adams

The reader naturally takes the second line as an introduction to the next quotation from Adams: the declaration of faith in providence to which Pound adds his quotation from Adolph Hitler. In fact it represents Pound's recognition that he had wrongly identified the first letter. He now indicates that the words "I said nothing etc." came from a "letter to Chase [not to his wife] from John Adams." Of course Pound could have clarified the identities of the recipients either by striking the line "wrote J. A. to his wife" or, since the succeeding mention of providence does appear in a letter to Adams's wife, by reversing this line with the one following. His failure to do either suggests a superstitious attachment to anything he had put on paper.

Whatever the explanation, the three lines in question are incoherent. As for the other three lines, which supposedly offer "an image of the quality of Adams's perceptions" and demonstrate the "superior immediacy" of Pound's "method," these involve equally embarrassing confusions on Kenner's part. [Kenner's second three lines come from Canto 68 (the last of these offers a good example of the end-line runover previously described):

> 'forward young man' wrote the critic
>   on an unsigned J. A. (J. A. being then 53 and vice
>   president)

Here Pound has again confused Charles Francis Adams's presentation. The quoted phrase is a comment by Adams himself about a reviewer of Adams's work *Discourses on Davila*. On the page of the biography from which Pound quotes, Charles Francis explains that Adams wrote the *Discourses* when he was vice-president. Elsewhere in the edition Charles Francis prints the text of the work and appends as footnotes John Adams's marginal comments made when he reread his book in 1804 and 1812. It is one of these comments, made in 1812, that Pound is quoting. In it Adams recalls the review of *Davila* by the "forward young man." Presumably the review was unsigned.

It is impossible to make out any of this from Pound's lines. But do the Poundians admit experiencing any difficulties? Not at all. Kenner finds everything perfectly lucid, and writes as follows:

> Characteristic turns of speech and the torsos of quoted sentences are here built into an image of the quality of Adams' perceptions and the nature of his concern for definition. The superior immediacy of this method over prose panegyric (an immediacy exemplified in the richly informative anecdote of

the critic who wrote "Forward young man" on an anonymous vice-presidential document) is its ample justification for the reader who is willing to go slowly and ponder.

Of course there was no such young man or document, since the critic was the young man himself, and the comment was Adams's—made years after he had been vice-president.] Yet if Kenner has imbibed more misinformation about Adams and American history than the other Poundians it is because he has read the Adams cantos with more care than they. Thus his list of important figures in the *Cantos*—"the great Emperors, the brothers Adams, Jefferson, Odysseus . . ."—evidently derives from the misleading line "But where the devil this brace of Adamses sprung from!" Out of context, as Pound quotes it, the phrase suggests two brothers, especially as Pound mentions "John's bro, the sheriff" in the first line of the same canto. But in fact neither of Adams's brothers achieved prominence. The brace of Adamses referred to is John and his cousin Samuel Adams, who appears frequently in the Adams cantos section but cannot be construed as one of its heroes. While one suspects the Poundians who follow Kenner of disingenuousness in avoiding comment on the Adams cantos, of Kenner it can at least be said that he truly believes in the coherence of Pound.

Kenner's misreadings tend to involve confusions about Charles Francis Adams. When one understands how Pound used Charles Francis's edition of *The Works of John Adams,* the continuing high reputation of the history cantos becomes suspect in a different way. For, more remarkable than Kenner's original praise for the Adams cantos has been the persistence of others in honoring them—and this despite their lack of method having been revealed in 1955. In the *Pound Newsletter,* the precursor of *Paideuma,* William Vasse wrote, "Even when reworking the material to some extent [Pound] has remained faithful to the spirit of the original. . . . except for a few editorial interpolations by Pound, it all does come from these works and is almost invariably arranged in the same chronological sequence as its source." The familiar obscurity of Poundians on the cantos here serves the purpose of concealment. Vasse implies that Pound used numerous "works" at the same time as he reports that Pound used but a single "source," *The Works of John Adams.* Then at the end of his sentence he mutedly reveals the key to it all: the Adams cantos sec-

tion is "almost invariably arranged in the same chronological sequence as its source." This means that Pound did *not* employ the devices of chronological time-shift and rearrangement that supposedly
account for his obscurity.

The fact is that the shifts in chronology and point of view in the
Adams cantos are the results of Pound's following the exact order of
Charles Francis Adams's *Works*. In this edition, after the first, biographical volume by Charles Francis, succeeding volumes contain
Adams's writings by type: diary and autobiography (combined to
produce a continuous narrative), political writings, public letters,
private letters. Pound went volume by volume, copying extracts as he
turned the pages. Far from reordering the materials, with a few tri-
fling exceptions he copied them in strict page order. The inevitable result of this slavish procedure is the confusing disarray of chronology
and point of view that led to Kenner's misreadings. (In contrast, the
earlier American history cantos do not seem to employ the supposed
method of chronological rearrangement because they follow works
organized in chronological order.)

By starting with the first volume, the biography, one reads Adams's
life as told by Charles Francis. One then goes on, beginning in the
second volume, to a mixture of Adams's diary account with his auto-
biographical recollections; next to his early political essays and Revolutionary writings; and then to his late works on government. After
these, one returns to the middle part of Adams's life as seen in his
official correspondence. Finally, one goes over the same middle period in personal letters, which continue, through the tenth volume,
into old age. Now, it might be argued that these materials appear in a
fortuitous thematic arrangement. But Pound obscures even this by
passing from one genre to another of Adams's writings without
warning. He never indicates whether he is quoting from the biography, from letters by or to Adams, from contemporary diary impressions, or from the recollections of old age. In a rare instance of in-
dicating a transition he supplies the word *dash:*

88 battalions, September,
dash had already formed lucrative connections in Paris

Here the first line comes from part 1 of Adams's autobiography,
which gives an account of the Continental Congress, and the second

from part 2 of his autobiography, in which he gives an account of his diplomatic service in Europe.

Elsewhere Pound goes from one volume to the next, and from diary to letters to quotations within quotations without so much as the cryptic word *dash*. By failing to do any more than quote the lines as they come along he leaves behind an indistinguishable welter of points of view. In the case of Kenner's misreadings the point of view is that of Charles Francis Adams, not John Adams (Kenner believed that the Adams cantos were "taken from the correspondence of John Adams"). Charles Francis offers varying perspectives on Adams's career throughout the *Works,* quoting in footnotes Adams himself, contemporaries, historians, and sometimes offering his own remarks or excerpts from relevant documents. All of these, too, are run into the Adams cantos without differentiation whenever Pound happens to be copying from the bottom of a page and hence from a footnote. The *Works* is a model of organizational clarity, but handled in this way it becomes an untranslated Rosetta stone, except that the Rosetta stone had clearly marked divisions among its three sections.

William Vasse's revelation of Pound's page-turning use of Adams's *Works,* although obscurely phrased, has been read and understood by Poundians after him. Yet, all who show familiarity with Vasse's essay accept his interpretation of the results. "Adams' most important actions," he writes,

> . . . are made recurrent. Adams' mission to Holland to secure allies and money for the colonies is presented first by a statement of the mission's results (p. 92); the results are again stated (p. 122) but now in the more expanded, less official form of John Adams' diary; the documents of the mission are then presented (pp. 146–152) to show how that result was attained; and finally Adams' own estimation of his mission is recorded. . . . The same method of restatement is used to focus attention upon all Adams' most important activities.

Aside from being implausible, this analysis neglects the fact that Pound himself did not subscribe to the notion of restatement. At the front of the Adams cantos volume he offered a table of contents that, contrary to Vasse, claims a strictly chronological presentation of

Adams's life. Though Pound of course wrote no such thing in the Adams cantos, the repetitions which occur in the *Works* made it possible for him selectively to make such a table. Neither Pound nor his followers, then, offer a true picture of the contents of the Adams cantos.

That picture is amply provided in Frederick Sanders's *John Adams Speaking,* which brings together "the lines of the poem and Pound's sources in a way that permits a reader to see for himself what relationship exists between them." Marvelous to report, no irony is intended here. For Sanders, too, finds a structure of "thematic repetitions" in the Adams cantos, and reports that he is working on a book that will demonstrate this in an "elaborate study of each one of the 'Adams Cantos.'" [This book has never appeared.]*

Sanders has nothing to say about Kenner's misreadings but does note some of Pound's. Vasse had compiled a list of fifty errors in the Adams cantos; to them Sanders adds ninety-nine of his own. (These, however, do not include the misreadings and misidentifications that led Kenner astray.) When Pound uses "Imperative" for Adams's "impracticable," Sanders points out, "Pound's reader would have every reason to form just the opposite impression [from the truth]." Nevertheless Sanders believes that Pound's errors raise no more than the "matter of judgment" concerning "whether a particular textual deviation is to be taken as an error or as an example of the way the poet has adapted his sources to his art." Understandably, Sanders does not speculate on those errors, clearly not typographical, which pointlessly reverse the meanings of passages, change dates, or wrongly identify writers and recipients of letters. The lack of pattern in these suggests intellectual breakdown; indeed, Pound's only consistency is in a greater tendency to miscopy when a passage concerns money.

For Sanders the triumphant demonstration of Pound's art occurs

* Poundians who write on the Adams cantos now use Sanders's key to the *Works* of John Adams. But their essays continue to profess finding a coherent pattern based on what one of them terms a method of "documentary collage." It has grown increasingly evident that numerous errors similar to those in the Adams cantos appear throughout Pound's *Cantos.* One Poundian critic lists some eight hundred errors in the first thirty cantos alone. As one of its chapter titles, Christine Froula's *To Write Paradise: Style and Error in Pound's* Cantos (1984), a work of Poundian apologetics, uses "The Pound Error," a pun on Hugh Kenner's *The Pound Era.*

in Canto 70 when a passage is quoted out of the chronological order of John Adams's *Works*. There are exactly two such instances in the Adams cantos, both in number 70. One might ask why, if these were intentional, Pound made only two such departures. His failure elsewhere to do what Sanders praises here implies an indictment of all but these half dozen lines of the Adams cantos. But Sanders does not reveal that there are only two cases in point. He discusses the second as representative of Pound's method throughout.

What Pound actually did in Canto 70 is evident from a revealing line at the end of Canto 69: "vignette *in margine*"—vignette in the margin. Evidently Pound ran across and used a marginal comment by the previous owner of his book. He either added lines of his own to the comment or translated it into Poundian ("ov the 64 members ov the House ov reppyzentativs"). The historically knowledgeable content of the marginal vignette passage, for which Sanders is unable to find a source, rules out the possibility of its being Pound's own. Evidently he simply continued copying from his margin through the beginning of Canto 70. The quotation there which appears to be the result of turning forward one volume is far more likely to have come from this same margin than from Pound's own industry.

There is a touching affinity among Pound, Adams, and the anonymous author of the lines in the margin. All three display a familiar type of lonely and isolated American crankiness and all three are eccentric annotators of obscure books. In his old age Adams filled volumes with marginalia. Pound, like him an isolato in old age, wrote pages of cantos that at the most generous estimate might be classed as a primitive kind of marginalia. Insofar as Pound had any grasp of Adams's character it unfortunately came from Charles Francis Adams's biography and interpretive notes, both of which figure copiously in the Adams cantos. In these Adams is presented as a figure of marmoreal probity: the unsmiling public man Charles Francis thought it his duty to make his grandfather appear. Yet on the evidence of the *Works*, if one ignores Charles Francis, a more interesting John Adams of wayward passion can be discerned. Thus, as far as one can make out, Pound never perceived the affinities between himself and Adams. Needless to say, neither did he present a new image of Adams unknown to historians. (Here I should note that I was alerted to Pound's probable use of marginalia partly by *John Adams*

and the Prophets of Progress by Zoltan Haraszti, a brilliant compilation
of Adams's marginalia, and partly by the Poundianly vituperative
marginalia in my own edition of Charles Francis's *Works of John
Adams*.)

The Adams cantos stand as a representative case of the excesses of
modernism, whose dogmas have shielded them from critical scrutiny. While the doctrine of the separation of art from life has pro-
tected their crackbrained and vicious ideas, the concurrent mythology of the artist has made Pound's life and these ideas appear as
guarantees of poetic excellence. The modern writer, insofar as he
appears as the alienated holder of unpopular opinions, and insofar as
his works are unpleasant, obscure, and insulting, has the critical
advantage. That his life and art might display these characteristics
without the accompaniment of poetic achievement is hardly to be
imagined. Of course a definitive analysis of Pound's state of mind
during the 1930s will have to await a thorough biographical study.
But in the meantime the evidence points to intellectual and poetic
decline below the level of respectability, along with signs of mental
breakdown. If the mindlessness of the Adams cantos has not been
generally recognized, their impenetrability has been evident to any
non-Poundian who has troubled to read them. Yet, instead of taking
their lack of sense as continuous with Pound's political rantings, intelligent critics have labored to excuse the politics and deceive themselves about the poetry.

Partisan Review, no. 1, 1977

LITERARY
CRITICISM

THE DECLINE
OF CRITICISM

=====

THE FAILED CULTURAL revolu-
tion of the 1960s proved remarkably successful in its assault on the
university, and especially on the humanities. In fact, the contempt
for learning and authority that marked the 1960s eventually penetrated the thinking of academics to the point where they became its
agents. In the meantime, a new attack, this one directed against intellectual discourse itself, has been undertaken by a group of critics
deeply influenced by contemporary French philosophers. This time,
academics in the humanities have hardly reacted. Practitioners of the
new literary critical movement in question are divided over its precise definition, as well as over what it should be called. *Revisionist
criticism* has been suggested, and also the French-derived term *de-
constructivism*. [This was the situation in 1977, before *deconstruction*
replaced the other terms.]

From different points of view and following various logics, practitioners of revisionist criticism—Harold Bloom and his Yale colleagues Geoffrey Hartman, J. Hillis Miller, Paul de Man, and Jacques
Derrida are among the best-known proponents—all manage to call
into question the common assumption that language is a dependable
means of communication. They attempt to show that both literature
and criticism are inevitably rife with ambiguities. Given the tendency
of the reader or listener to confuse his own prejudices with the message being sent, they argue that all uses of words prove to be no less
uncertain than the most abstruse poetry.

The tenuousness of language to which these critics refer has always been appreciated. What is being claimed for the first time,

43

though, is that we must give up any illusion that we can gain a clear understanding of the written word. The paradoxes of communication, formerly regarded as challenges to the wits of writer and reader, are now considered primary, absolute bars to any degree of certainty whatsoever.

It follows from these new propositions that the moral attitude of a given work of fiction can in no case be made clear, least of all through the kind of explicit assertion favored by champions of traditional values in fiction. John Gardner's vigorous unequivocalness, for example, becomes by definition no less ambiguous than any other statements about meaning and morality. The issue compromising academic criticism today is simply whether it is possible to mean what one says and to convey that meaning to others. Anyone wishing to answer in the affirmative must begin by confronting the new language of indeterminism.

This language, as it develops, has surprising similarities to that currently spoken by instructors in college classrooms throughout the United States. Here, too, certainty and piety of all kinds are systematically undermined in favor of a universal relativism of values and judgment. Just as the revisionists are led to reduce the act of criticism to a given critic's subjective preference, so do professors relegate judgment of all sorts to the students' subjective preferences. The approach is akin to positing as truth one's responses on the psychologists' Thematic Apperception Test.

College professors thus share a skepticism about art and knowledge, the intellect and culture, not only with revisionist critics but with anti-intellectuals outside academe as well. In the end, from this point of view nothing makes any sense; everything is relative, anyway; one person's opinion is as good as another's; moral distinctions are useless. They all reduce to power and desire—to my own opinion, the way I feel, what seems right to me. The diverse adherents of this philosophy, whether they be anti-intellectuals, revisionist critics, or professors at colleges and universities prestigious and obscure, come down to being part of the same descent into solipsism.

Two recent books give witness to the seductions of an unwitting academy by the assumptions of indeterminism over the past twenty years. In *Literature against Itself: Literary Ideas in Modern Society,* the critic Gerald Graff analyzes the "deconstruction" of literary discourse by revisionist theoreticians. In *New Readings vs. Old Plays: Recent Trends in the Reinterpretation of English Renaissance Drama,* Richard Levin exposes the fatuities of conventional academic criticism in an analysis that makes one begin to understand the decline of the university.

As in any subject, a certain amount of nonsense has always been evident in Richard Levin's field of English Renaissance drama and Shakespearean studies. The excesses have been exposed and parodied, especially where they resemble practices in other areas of English studies. More than one critic, for example, has laughed over the academic tendency to treat fictional characters as "Christ figures." Inevitably, any wound suffered in a book will be likened by some commentator to the Crucifixion. A fictional character who is going to die, moreover, had better not eat anything before his demise lest his act be identified as an allusion to the Last Supper. This sort of foolishness, which is more common than one might suppose, is ordinarily treated as an "abuse" of critical method, and not as an indictment of it. But Levin demonstrates that "abuses" of this sort are persistent in his field, that they are systematic, and that to a significant extent they have become the basis of thinking about Shakespeare and his era. Had Levin set out with the intention of discrediting English studies in general, he could not have chosen a more representative corner of the discipline. For Shakespearean criticism has always included in itself the major issues of critical method.

Levin shows that Renaissance literary interpretation has resolved itself into three formulaic approaches. The first concentrates on the themes of plays, the second searches for ironies, and the third, which pretends to be historical, reinterprets according to what Elizabethan and Jacobean audiences are supposed to have felt and believed. Critics who adopt one or more of these approaches come to believe that the one thing a play does not mean is what it appears to mean. Nevertheless, despite the failure of all previous interpreters to recognize this fact, the new academic readings prove always to be successful, and to render superfluous all previous understandings of the play, character, or scene under examination. In one article after another in the most prestigious academic journals, the shared experiences of audiences and readers for some three hundred years are regularly overthrown. How such startling developments can have been taking place for the past twenty years without being reported in the press, let alone making news in the academic world, is a question in itself, and one that I will return to.

In the academic criticism of old plays the most popular themes seem to be love, corruption, honor, and especially "Time." Pairs of themes are still more common, with the list being led by order and disorder, love and war, art versus nature, reason and imagination, and the most popular of all, appearance and reality. To be sure, the thematic importance of Hamlet's words "I know not 'seems'" in the first act of the play is undeniable. With this remark Hamlet initiates a series of variations on the riddle or theme of appearance and reality. Is there really a ghost? Is he trustworthy? How best deal with Rosencrantz and Guildenstern's deceptive sycophancy? And how take the traveling actors' false yet true imitation of emotion?

However, just as the deceitfulness of language is exaggerated into metaphysics by the revisionists, so the Renaissance specialists elevate themes into systems of infinite complexity. Ranging among the themes with unaccountable ease, the critics affirm that they have been able to identify and explain complexities completely different from anything their predecessors or even their contemporaries have ever suspected. One, commenting on rival interpretations of *Troilus and Cressida,* not long ago explained that "the play, as I read it, is not 'about' love and war, or love and honor, or policy and emotion. . . . Rather it deals with the single problem of corruption and its causes." Soon afterward this critic was dismissed by another, who confidently identified "Time" as the conclusive theme of the play. That critic was then superseded by yet another, who reinstated "the corruptive spirit."

This sort of sterile formulation of literature made a plausible cause of despair for the English professor, Butley, in Simon Gray's play of the same name a few years ago. As Butley reads aloud the titles of his students' papers—"Hate and Redemption, Pity and Terror, Sin and Salvation"—he grows comically but seriously outraged and depressed (over the profession, not the students). One might argue in favor of the approach to literature so depressing to Butley that the proliferation of thematic formulas is evidence of a lively academic debate, but nothing could be further from the truth. Debate presumes the possibility of agreement, whereas the thematists have not the slightest interest in arriving at either truth or consensus. Instead, their practice depends on a constant, endless, and total disagreement over the identity of the themes in any given play.

The disagreements among thematists thus quite definitively undermine any claim they might have to be taken seriously. From another point of view, though, their excesses deserve recital for the light they throw on the present state of literary studies, both in the academic journals and in the classroom. It is important that the readers of a respectable scholarly journal have been warned against the "misleading impression" that *Othello* "is about jealousy." And that one critic is barely willing to admit that the same play significantly concerns Othello and Desdemona: "Since I see the unresolvable appearance-reality dualism as the center of the *Othello* design, I regard Emilia-Iago as the play's central relationship." Such readings are regularly applied throughout English Renaissance drama. Levin's other categories of dramatic criticism—the ironic and the historical—yield equally fatuous absurdities.

For the ironist, virtually all heroes are flawed and all happy endings false. Hamlet, for example, is "a soul lost in damnable error . . . a serpent-like scourge . . . a profane fool." The marriage scene at the end of the comedy *A Midsummer Night's Dream* conveys "a ghastly reminder" of death—that is if we have read the sources and know that one of the marriages is reported in legend to have produced a child who later died. "Historical" critics reveal that the secret meaning of a given play lies in its having been composed for a special occasion—usually a supposed performance before King James. With this key it can be shown that certain characters actually represent the king, and that commonsense understandings of the dialogue miss a host of esoteric references to the king's writings and ideas. In fact, there is absolutely no evidence for these "occasionalist" claims, which recall the semimystical maunderings of the anti-Stratfordians—that lunatic fringe of readers who assert that Shakespeare of Stratford is not the author of the plays.

It is difficult to say which is harder to believe: that the claims of historical occasionalism can actually have been published, or that their significance, which would be spectacular if true, has gone largely unnoticed. In fact, as with the attempts to assimilate one character after another to the Christ image, a number of scholars have attacked occasionalism. But for the most part, along with thematism and ironism, it continues to reign unchallenged.

If someone were to take the unprecedented step of reading the criticism of the past twenty years with a view to gaining a perspective on, say, *Romeo and Juliet,* what would be the result? That the pair would be exposed as anything but star-crossed lovers may be easily guessed in advance. But this is not all. One would learn that Romeo, who never achieves "true love" according to Saint Paul's definition, something he should have done, "took up the purchase of illegal drugs (which ultimately caused his own death)." Romeo, in fact, is "close to a mass murderer." In the character of Juliet, "perversion" and the "rawness" of "sexual hunger" prevail. (In this she resembles Othello's Desdemona, who according to another critic "shrinks from the reality of the whore within her.") An unnatural, indecent, sinful girl, Juliet must be condemned along with Romeo for the blasphemy of committing suicide. In the end, the study of "history" teaches us that "the average audience of *Romeo and Juliet* would have regarded the behavior of the young lovers as deserving everything they got."

The vulgarity of this conclusion, along with its fractured grammar, may give the impression that such opinions as it typifies are uncommon exceptions—the work of obscure hacks in the profession. But the abuses gathered by Levin have been committed by critics at every level of competence and reputation. Moreover, while they have been ignored in general, such readings have gained respectability and even fame within the specialty of Renaissance and Shakespearean criticism. Clearly, the entire profession bears responsibility for creating an atmosphere that has permitted such work to establish itself.

But let us return to the idea of seriously attempting to synthesize the new academic readings in order to learn something about a particular play, and to the related mystery of why their startling newness has never been reported to the world. By now it must be apparent that the explanation in both cases is that for the most part this criticism is simply not read—and with good reason. It is ignored not only by newspaper reporters but also by cultivated readers, by professors of English, and even by Renaissance and Shakespearean specialists, including thematists, ironists, and occasionalists themselves.

The same lack of interest in criticism prevails not just in Renaissance scholarship but throughout the profession. Although surveys like Levin's remain to be written on the other specialties within English studies, evidence of what would be uncovered is suggested whenever an academic bewails the so-called publish-or-perish imperative and the proliferation of publications that it breeds. "It is impossible to keep up with work in the field," the professional journals repeatedly declare. Either because academic criticism cannot be read, then, or because no one wishes to read it, professionals in the field, by their own admission, do not keep up with its progress. How, then, have they muddled through? Very simply by ignoring their peers, while remaining secure in the knowledge that by doing so they miss nothing of importance.

Levin believes that a tendency to debunk is built into each of the approaches that he has anatomized. But the devaluation of values that they share can as easily be seen as part of a wider phenomenon: the erosion of certainty about what is true and right. It is significant, for example, that an article (not mentioned by Levin) can have been published with the title "In Defense of Goneril and Regan." Nor is its sympathy for two of literature's most despicable villains the worst example of academic wrongheadedness on record. Renaissance criticism has strayed so far from ordinary human impulses that most of it would hardly lead one to suspect that characters, actions, and feelings have anything whatsoever to do with the theater. Characters are made into vehicles of ideas; when they speak it is to "debate" and "discuss" the abstractions that are taken to be the real business of the plays. Marriages are "symbolic," and tragic endings convey no pain, even to the protagonists.

Students introduced to this universe learn to adopt the attitude toward it of their professors. They come to treat literary talk, that is, as a rarefied discourse that does not have to be tested against ordinary experience. Yet this does not necessarily insulate them from either the cynicism or the nihilism of their professors' critical dogma, for covert assumptions reach students more surely than explicit philosophies. Academic criticism starts with the assumption that there are no such things as admirable human beings, unequivocally admirable acts, or truly pure motives for acts. To prove that these do not exist, every conceivable method of questioning motives is employed. (Here the assumption conveyed is that the end justifies the means.) As Levin shows, the close analysis of character has resolved itself into the use of "character assassination," guilt by association, and innuendo. In view of this debased morality it would on the whole seem safest to keep one's college-age children away from the intellectual influence of most English professors.

In retrospect, the rise of literary revisionism may be taken as a reaction to the bankruptcy of conventional academic criticism. Yet revisionism arrives not as a cure but as a consequence: a kind of *reductio ad absurdum*. The revisionists have presented themselves as opponents of the Establishment, while in turn being rejected by most academics. Nevertheless, the systematic dismissal of common sense by conventional critics and the programmatic uncertainty of revisionists have much in common. As long ago as the 1950s, when some critics began to have misgivings about the new readings discussed by Levin, the complaint was raised that "misreadings" were becoming the norm. Similarly, in revisionist criticism the first consequence of calling discourse itself into question is the proposition that all criticism amounts to misreading, and thus one reading is as legitimate as another.

Seizing upon this apparently inescapable conclusion with an infectious panache, Harold Bloom elevated it into a leading principle of revisionist criticism in the early 1970s, but he was only giving a local habitation—Yale—and a name—his own—to what had already become standard academic practice. Here it was, then, that the quiet decline of academic criticism reached its logical dead end. For as Bloom and others claimed, since misreading is inevitable, the best critics will be those who voluntarily admit their fallibility. By embracing misreading as their starting point, they will be liberated from the constraints formerly imposed on critics by their naive faith in the possibility of achieving objectivity. Not only is certainty unattainable, but the only virtue lies in abandoning the attempt to achieve it.

A certain glamour has attached itself to the revisionist enterprise insofar as it represents the latest literary insurgency. On the other hand, it was begun by middle-aged academics whose style and manner are nothing if not magisterial. As a result the charges leveled by opponents—of self-indulgent subjectivism, of thesis-ridden obscurity, of a purposely evasive use of terminology, and of an attempt to supplant the artist by shifting attention to the drama in one's own thought—are commonly received with a patronizing air. And of course if one makes the mistake of charging that the revisionist is in error, he need only respond that the charge is quite correct, since that is exactly what he had in mind.

The tone of debate over the issues was caught a year ago by a student reporter for the Columbia University *Spectator* when he described "a blistering but dignified debate on the nature of modern literary criticism which featured leading experts in the field expounding on such topics as 'perceptual closures,' 'semantic gestalt,' 'undecidable significations,' and 'evolving sequences of false surmises.'" The revisionist tone must be infectious, for the antirevisionist, humanist critic M. H. Abrams was reported to have "called for a return to 'traditional hermeneutical' readings through which interpretation would rest on 'certain consensual regularities' rather than with 'the text as such.'"

Theoretically, there can be no refutation of the utter skepticism that underlies revisionism. The literary theorist Wayne C. Booth makes this point in *Critical Understanding: The Powers and Limits of Pluralism,* his book on literary disagreement. In the face of radical skepticism, he writes, we must retreat and admit that our confidence in making sense and communicating it to one another is based on faith. But luckily, he adds, few pursue the challenge. Gerald Graff, in contrast, has recognized that revisionist criticism offers exactly such a challenge, and he has attempted to meet it. Graff shows first of all that in practice, revisionism adopts a facile metaphysic. Its practitioners keep showing that because art, like criticism, cannot know its object (the world), all fictions are essentially about nothing more than themselves. But this conclusion always proceeds from an unargued certainty about the futility of knowing, and so degenerates into a new kind of critical cant.

But revisionists do assume that they know the nature of literature: they are certain that it is reflexive. When they proclaim that the novel is "a self-consciously fictive construction," they are themselves assuming knowledge of a certain version of reality, albeit a putatively confusing one; and when they assert that the novel reflects the world's unknowableness they are actually positing the oldest literary theory of all: Aristotle's mimesis, or imitation. As it turns out, then, they both know reality and believe that literature imitates it, so that they live with a more serene confidence about the way things are than most people do.

To prove that the revisionists believe in reality and certainty despite their disclaimers hardly begins to meet their challenge. For theirs is not merely an academic tendency, but rather a movement with political sources and aims. To understand these it is necessary to recall the short history of literary radicalism in America. In the 1930s, literary radicals from the genteel Granville Hicks to the fiery Michael Gold championed proletarian literature and criticism. Writers were supposed to write about the working class and to conclude their books with uplifting spectacles of labor on strike; critics were supposed to praise those works that came closest to this model. After the Depression and the Second World War such simplemindedness was rejected, and overtly radical literature and criticism fell into disrepute among intellectuals on the Left. Then in the 1960s, much to the surprise of the Old Left, the radical-proletarian prescriptions of the 1930s began to be voiced again.

This time, with somewhat greater subtlety, writers were urged to depict the lives of America's downtrodden and of its minorities. Such subjects as these were assumed to harbor an oblique summons to action. But in the 1960s, as in the 1930s, literary radicals continued to separate themselves from their opponents by championing realism. Realistic literature showed life as it is, and so provided the basis for political action. Other literary forms, such as idealism and fantasy, made such action less likely by distorting reality. In the radical formula, to depart from reality was to serve the ruling class.

Through revisionist criticism the cultural radicals of the 1970s have completely reversed the assumptions and program set forth in the 1960s. The revisionists begin and end by dismissing social reality. It is, they argue, nothing but an artificial category. For them, reality in literature serves rather than threatens the powers that be. Depicted in literature, "bourgeois reality" makes life as it is appear inevitable and unchangeable, thereby encouraging acquiescence in the capitalist status quo so that it functions as a mechanism of political control. It follows that the revolutionary act lies not in practicing socialist realism but rather in deconstructing reality according to the revisionist formula.

As in traditional radical politics, this new "politics of anti-realism," as Graff terms it, assigns revolutionary tasks to art and criticism. "By refusing to hold a mirror up to nature, by exploding the very idea of a stable 'nature,' art strikes at the psychological and epistemological bases of the ruling order." In cooperation with art, Graff's synopsis continues, "criticism ought to explode the professional academic myths of 'the work itself,' the 'intention' of the author, and the determinate nature of textual meaning."

While this new program is far more sophisticated than those that it replaced, its complete turnabout with regard to objectivity and reality has not been accomplished without a sacrifice of logic. For the practice of deconstruction in criticism has no actual connection with the political revolution that it superficially imitates. Having abandoned a reliable definition of reality, those who wish to change the present organization of society have left themselves with no ground to stand on. They are as doomed to inconsequence, one might say, as their predecessors of the 1960s were with their politics of symbolic protest in the streets. And yet Graff has not sufficiently taken into account the success of 1960s cultural politics. Despite its failure to achieve a revolution, that politics nevertheless effected wide-reaching changes in sensibility. Similarly, while the present assault on reality may also fail politically, its subversion of common sense and discourse cannot be easily dismissed.

From this point of view, the critiques offered by both Graff and Levin, though well taken, are inadequate. Graff calls for the championing of objectivity and reality. Levin advocates more stringent peer review of scholarly articles and a return to historical criticism, proposals that mandate information instead of speculation. But the fact that a consensus about the nature of history and reality can have been abandoned in the first place argues against the likelihood of its being restored.

It is hardly reassuring to witness Levin's being repeatedly forced to the necessity of pointing out that if Shakespeare and his contemporaries did not mean what they seem to be saying, there was nothing to prevent them from making themselves clear to their audiences. As for Graff, once he has had to point out that "the very notions of understanding, definition, explanation, and 'point of view' have come to seem suspect," and that "the term 'meaning' itself, as applied not only to art but to more general experience, has joined 'truth' and 'reality' in the class of words which can no longer be written unless apologized for by inverted commas," he can hardly hope for reform through the agency of sweet reason. He may demonstrate that even though language colors our perceptions and our attempts to convey them to others, we nevertheless do apprehend the world and successfully communicate it to others. But the very necessity that has put him in this position argues against the likelihood of a reformation in literary thinking. When one is forced to elaborate the most elementary canons of reason and common sense, the situation may be described as already all but hopeless.

The malaise within English studies, like the university's other complaints, has been described as a temporary crisis in the evolution of a venerable and necessary institution. Yet it should be remembered that both the university and its departments have not always existed, and that during their tenure they have not always served as indispensable channels for the flow of the cultural stream. Less than a hundred years ago, English studies hardly existed. Moreover, when they replaced classical studies, that discipline passed quietly into desuetude while hardly anyone noticed. It is not at all inconceivable, given the history of the humanities, that English studies, though at present the seemingly irreplaceable guardian of the Western cultural tradition, should decline to the current marginal status of the classics.

From the revival of classical culture by Renaissance humanists through most of the nineteenth century, classical studies reigned supreme in British culture. Then, just when it seemed clear that an Englishman wishing to enter colonial administration, politics, or the professions absolutely required a classical education, it developed that he could uphold the empire just as well if he majored in English. Somehow the values of the classical tradition and the humanist spirit could now be transmitted through the study of literature in the modern European languages, especially one's own.

At present this means of transmission prevails. But the arts and literature have appeared to be flourishing in past epochs when in fact they were on the verge of extinction, and so it may be with literature and criticism today. For in the decay of cultural institutions, the moment of demise cannot be pinpointed until well after it has passed. Thus, the poetry and scholarship produced for centuries after the fall of Rome seemed to preserve the classical tradition until they were relegated to the status of a footnote to that tradition. And as for the empire itself, certain Europeans went on living in their villas during the period, unaware that the life they associated with Rome was a posthumous one.

If it is difficult to pinpoint exactly when an institution has reached the end of its vigorous life, it is relatively easy to detect the signs of its preparation for inconsequence. These are always internal. It is not the attacks from without that prove crucial—not assaults by Goths or cultural revolutionaries—but the ways that the guardians of the tradition themselves behave. In academe, they prove to have abandoned the citadel years before it came under attack. As a result, the professors' uncoerced embrace of absurdity and inconsequence amounts to the surrender of their role in the transmission of culture before a shot was fired.

Harper's, October 1979

THE POLITICS OF
DECONSTRUCTION

===============

IN THE PAST FEW YEARS decon-
structionist literary criticism, after enjoying a seeming exemption
from close scrutiny by outsiders, has been subjected to a number of
searching critiques. As a result, the intellectual implications of the
movement have begun to be understood, and it has lost its sacrosanct
aura. Deconstruction has been challenged on philosophical grounds
for its dismissal of traditional Western thought and identified as a
threat both to literary criticism and discourse in general. Yet among
the now numerous critiques of deconstruction, there has been virtually no mention of what is arguably the movement's most significant
feature: its origins in radical politics.

These origins continue to go unmentioned despite Gerald Graff's
1978 essay, "The Politics of Realism," and his subsequent "Textual
Leftism," which together showed that deconstruction amounted to a
politically inspired attack on the philosophical underpinnings of
bourgeois society. The basis of this attack was the recognition by political radicals of the degree to which certain common assumptions—
that we live in an objectively knowable world and that we are able to
communicate its nature to one another—make possible the day-to-
day operation of society. The radicals put it that bourgeois society
actually controls its populace and prevents revolution not so much
by force as through its control of concepts such as these. Realistic
writing, for example, even when it is "radical in content," serves this
society, as Graff explains the radical argument, merely by employing
"formal modes of perception that [are] conventional and reaction-

ary." These modes lure the reader away from revolution by securing his acceptance of the world as it is.

It follows from this analysis that whoever helps to undermine the bourgeois perception of reality strikes a politically revolutionary blow. To be sure, critics have been attracted to the deconstructionist mode from a variety of traditions and motives, many of them removed from politics. Yet in joining the assault on reason, they have willy-nilly lent themselves to the political agenda of deconstruction.

The aim of Marxist literary criticism has always been to make whatever contribution it could to the overthrow of bourgeois society. The first Marxist critics simply criticized that society through literature. Granville Hicks's *The Great Tradition* (1935) used American literature in particular. Its putative great American tradition was that of proletarian, revolutionary literature. Hicks searched the nineteenth century for writers in sympathy with the common man and critical toward business civilization. These he elevated and connected with the proletarian novels being written in the 1930s as a "fulfillment of the [radical] spirit" of the earlier literature. Together the old and new, he proclaimed, pointed to a revolutionary future.

The crudities of such an approach were apparent at the outset. Hicks's great, proletarian tradition was at best a minor strain in American literature; his approach, moreover, was hopelessly inadequate to deal with first-rate literature. Something more sophisticated was called for, and the continental theorist Georg Lukács supplied it. In *Studies in European Realism* (1948), he largely set aside the political intentions of the writer. Émile Zola, for example, may have been a "writer of the left," but he was less useful to revolution than the royalist, Balzac, whose work could be treated as an exposé of the rotten core of bourgeois society. Lukács's departure did not entirely alienate him from a critic such as Hicks, for in addition to sharing a revolutionary purpose, both championed realism. But Lukács recognized the need to write about art in terms that would satisfy the intellectual class with something more than the transposition of political slogans to literature. His ability to develop a respectably complex theory accounts for his current popularity among Marxist poststructuralists.

The still greater subtlety of deconstruction lies in its virtual abandonment of explicit politics. Radical ideas are no longer alluded to except through the invocation of certain apparently literary terms.

For example, works of literature that have come to make up the canon of accepted masterpieces are referred to by deconstructionists as "privileged texts," the implication being not only that these works hold a special position in literature, but also that because of this they deserve the same suspicion and resentment that a revolutionary would be expected to direct at social privilege.

In a similar way, other terms used in deconstruction mime revolutionary struggle, producing a symbolic drama in which a liberation struggle is conducted in the name of subjectivity and indeterminacy of meaning in the face of "authoritarian," "reactionary," "hierarchical," "tyrannical," "imperialistic," or "hegemonic" views of reality—terms that apply to any normative supposition that objective values or meanings exist. Whoever hews to fixed meanings is said to participate in an act of "control" in literature analogous to the control that the imperialist-bourgeois state supposedly imposes on the exploited and the downtrodden. The State of Letters is conceived of as a surrogate for the political state, and as the battle against both escalates, so too does the language of deconstruction. Thus Jacques Derrida assaults the putative controllers of bourgeois reality by saying that when it comes to critical discourse, "the police is always waiting in the wings to enforce linguistic conventions." And Roland Barthes declares that all language is "quite simply fascistic."

Most literary observers of deconstruction have contrived to ignore the unmistakably political thrust of such expressions. As a result, it was not until the early 1980s that the politics of deconstruction began to be made explicit—and then only by Marxists grown disenchanted with the alliance they had maintained with the movement. Thus Edward Said's criticism of the poststructuralists—the most prominent of whom are the deconstructionists—implied that these were critics who had always harbored politically revolutionary intentions. In Said's disappointed view, though, all of their attempts to be radical had acted only to "further solidify and guarantee the social structure and the culture that produced them." This formula of dismissal has been taken up increasingly by younger Marxists since it appeared in Said's *The World, the Text, and the Critic* in 1983, with the result that one of them could recently state that "the most current means for detecting the bankruptcy of a certain theory or method is to uncover its political blindness, its irrelevance to any program for 'radical social change.'"

One user of this formula—the British Marxist Terry Eagleton—praises deconstruction for having helped to "keep the revolution warm," but dismisses it all the same. Revealingly, he traces the origins of deconstruction to the failed revolutionism of the 1960s, most particularly the student uprising of 1968 in Paris. "Unable to break the structures of state power," he writes, literary critics sympathetic to the student movement developed in poststructuralism a movement that "found it possible instead to subvert the structures of language." For Roland Barthes in particular, he reports, the enemies of the student movement "became coherent belief systems of any kind."

In *Marxism and Deconstruction* (1982), Michael Ryan similarly pointed out that "deconstructive philosophy emerged at the same time as the New Left." Ryan gave it as his opinion that "deconstruction cannot be called a New Left philosophy," but continued (in what he considered to be terms of praise):

> Nevertheless it projects certain recognizably new leftish traits: an emphasis on plurality over authoritarian unity, a disposition to criticize rather than obey, a rejection of the logic of power and domination in all their forms, an advocation of difference against identity, and a questioning of state universalism. It goes one step further and argues for the flawed and structurally incomplete, if not contradictory, nature of all attempts at absolute or total philosophic systems.

No more than the symbolically revolutionary language of deconstruction itself has the forthrightness of this and other recent statements by Marxists breached the virtual gentlemen's agreement among critics not to mention the politics of deconstruction. Indeed, the philosopher John Searle omitted politics altogether from his persuasive refutation of deconstruction in *The New York Review of Books* in 1983. A year earlier in the same journal, Denis Donoghue came no closer to explicitness than ending his critique of deconstruction with the following, obscure afterthought: "And there is the politics of Deconstruction: like Structuralism, it is antibourgeois, and particularly hostile to the ego-psychology which a bourgeois ideology is supposed to offer its members as a consolation prize." Donoghue appears to comprehend the politics of deconstruction, but he does not quite reveal to the reader what they might be.

The few observers to speculate on whether deconstruction and Marxism are related to one another have tended to be dismissive. As a British critic put it, "deconstruction is so obviously anti-dialectical: how could it possibly join forces with 'dialectical materialism'?" (Despite this particular dismissal, English critics, writing as they do from within a considerably Marxified academic environment, are by and large far closer to the French than the Americans in their openness about the politics of deconstruction.) Writing in 1983, the American critic Robert Alter similarly asked if there was "some deep affinity between Deconstruction and political revolutionism." Not really, he decided. Derrida's announced radicalism must be regarded as no more than a common position in French intellectual circles. And while it is true that Jonathan Culler, the author of *On Deconstruction: Theory and Criticism after Structuralism,* the most frequently cited introduction to the subject, "in fact was an S.D.S. activist in the late '60s," he should not be regarded as a radical either, since for him "the last true revolution is feminism." From a theoretical point of view, Alter added, "it is hard to see how Deconstructive analysis, conceptually removed as it is from historical process, can address itself to concrete political realities." Of course it is exactly the point of deconstruction to circumvent concrete political realities in favor of another kind of assault on culture; furthermore, success or failure does not alter the nature of this decidedly political intention.

When one turns to American deconstruction, the political element is obscured because of a problem of definition. The movement in this country is understood originally to have comprised a core of members within the Yale University Department of English. But there remains considerable disagreement over how the department's members at the time—Harold Bloom, the late Paul de Man, Geoffrey Hartman, and J. Hillis Miller—should be described. It is often said that Bloom does not really practice deconstruction. Denis Donoghue has gone so far as to assert that the only American member of the Yale department who did was Paul de Man (Jacques Derrida was a regular but visiting member of the department), and that "Geoffrey Hartman is one of the most vigorous opponents of Deconstruction." On the other hand, when the Yale critics collaborated on a volume of their work in 1980, they titled it *Deconstruction and Criticism;* all of them, moreover, can be found listed in the bibliographies of deconstruction (as can Edward Said).

The problem of defining who is a deconstructionist is typical of the confusions that have prevented clear statements about the purposes of deconstruction. Yet it is not really necessary to puzzle over the differences among its practitioners. For the unnoticed fact is that most writing done under the name of poststructuralism and deconstruction concerns itself very little with the act of analysis itself. That act has been described by Vincent B. Leitch as the undermining of confidence in discourse through a technique of "repetition." As Leitch explains: "The deconstructive interpreter carefully traces and repeats certain elements in the text, which may include the figures, the concepts, or the motifs in a work. As he or she repeats the selected elements, the critic unleashes the disruptive powers inherent in all repetition." Having rendered the text before him inchoate, the deconstructive critic characteristically concludes that he has succeeded in exposing the naivete of the old uncertainties about writing: that authorial intent is communicated through the written word and that readers share a common experience of reading.

But has he actually done so? The truth is that one can read through the Yale critics—or through Edward Said, Roland Barthes, and Derrida—or one can read through the journals *Boundary, Critical Inquiry, Critical Texts, Diacritics, Enclitic, Georgia Review,* and *Glyph,* without finding more than a few stray lines that trouble to perform the deconstructive task described by Leitch. Instead, the vast preponderence of writing in the field concerns theory.

The virtual absence of practical criticism does not make deconstruction's claims any less challenging, but it does put them in perspective. Rather than testing particular poems or prose texts, as is sometimes made to seem the case, deconstruction challenges traditional views of literature through general propositions. Inasmuch as these propositions have been intimately bound up with politics from the beginning, one can hardly be said to understand them in the pure isolation with which deconstruction is treated by most literary critics.

When it comes to placing the Yale critics, it follows that their theoretical agreements are far more important than the often-mentioned variations among them. Thus Harold Bloom, whose relationship to deconstruction is usually said to be the most problematical of all, advances a personal theory of what he calls "misprision," which comes down to asserting that all interpretations of literature, including his own, are really misreadings. (Paul de Man, along with Stanley Fish of Johns Hopkins, holds that all readings are correct, which amounts to the same thing.) Like his colleagues, Bloom discusses his theory more than practices it. But more importantly, misprision is quite compatible with deconstruction's program of spreading indeterminacy.

Where does the theoretical compatibility of the Yale critics with deconstruction place them with respect to the radical politics of the original French deconstructionists? As we have seen, in the new Marxified climate of literary opinion deconstruction itself has been found politically wanting. As for Yale in particular, Jacques Derrida has expressed disappointment that his colleagues there have served "the dominant political and economic interests of American society." The Yale group, though, tends to be castigated not so much for failing to bring about social change as for not trying to do so in the first place. Thus Terry Eagleton has recently indicted the Yale critics for a reading of Derrida that "eradicates all traces of the political from his work." (On the other hand, Eagleton is willing to grant that Geoffrey Hartman "has explicitly repudiated such an accusation, and there is evidence that de Man believed himself to be a socialist.") Frank Lentricchia gets at what particularly annoys radicals about Yale when he criticizes Paul de Man for having "no *desire* to employ the literary in the redemptive work of social change" (italics added).

By refusing to acknowledge the politics of deconstruction, then, the Yale critics eventually disgusted the radicals. But the same refusal involved them in silence about the political uses to which their work was being put. Were they chiefly naive, self-deceived, or evasive about their place in the radical scheme of things? Whichever it was, by the 1980s explicit accounts by literary Marxists were making it impossible even for Yale any longer to ignore politics. Furthermore, American literary criticism in the 1980s grew to be at least as politicized as deconstruction had been at its inception in France in the 1960s. In fact, the politics of literary theory in America reached the point where William E. Cain could recently report with approval: "In literary theory circles, Marxism has acquired a special status and is now the predominant subject and system of belief in debates about the politics of interpretation. No one dares to utter a liberal doctrine."

Perhaps the most important result of Marxist dominance has been the demystification of deconstruction. Writing as a Marxist, Terry Eagleton is free to turn the tables and accuse deconstruction of the same authoritarianism that it routinely finds inherent in bourgeois criticism. Deconstructionists, writes Eagleton, exercise "the *privilege* of those who can afford not to know" and "the *authoritarian* abrasiveness of informing you that you do not know what you are saying" (italics added). More insultingly still, Eagleton writes that they deserve the Gramscian epithet "hegemonic," the ultimate in poststructuralist political damnation.

In the wake of such remarks, the critique of deconstruction from other, nonpolitical quarters has taken courage. One can now find in print, for example, vigorous denials of the doctrine that the imperfections of communication add up to chaos. Critics, while granting that no written communication is perfect, and that readers derive varying impressions from what they read, no longer accept that these circumstances justify concluding that the message can never get through. Substantially, it is now being said, we do understand one another. More generally, although it is undeniable that certain logical propositions can always be called into question, the French critics Foucault, Piaget, Barthes, Derrida, and others have no warrant, as Geoffrey Thurley puts it in his book *Counter-Modernism in Current Critical Theory* (1983), for asserting "that because some statements cannot be verified no statements can."

With arguments such as these on the one side, and the radical attack on the other, it is not difficult to predict the decline of deconstruction. But it would be a mistake either to regard deconstruction as a passing curiosity or to declare as Terry Eagleton does that deconstruction merely "cancels all the way through and leaves everything just as it was." Such conclusions may possibly be justified if one is measuring direct political results in the world at large. But from the more enduring perspective of ideas, things are by no means just as they were.

In the first place, deconstruction now reigns as the one prestige subject capable of drawing graduate students of literature to extracurricular study groups in literary theory, where the subject inevitably devolves into poststructuralism. Generations of such students by now have written dissertations and built careers either wholly or partly under the influence of deconstruction. The more nimble of them may prove able to step along to the next literary orthodoxy, but even these few will, in the normal way of academics, continue to transmit the concepts and techniques they absorbed in graduate school.

In the second place, deconstructionist attitudes, especially skepticism about the existence of any firm knowledge and the replacement of rationality by subjectivity, have spread beyond literary theory to virtually every corner of literary study. A recent book on the subject of scholarly biography, for example, calls on the researcher to depend on "an intuitive sense of his subject, although this often means the manipulation of data." Such "freedom from fact," we are informed, "has recently become celebrated by contemporary biographers as a new methodology."

Not only biographers are celebrating freedom from fact these days, but also scholars throughout the humanities and social sciences, while some theorists of science edge in the same direction. Thus deconstruction proves to have provided the philosophical justification for a broad movement away from Western objectivity and rationality. In this perspective it has to be judged a success, having helped to bring about a number of results in the intellectual world: a retreat to relativism of values; distaste for the assertion of either intellectual authority or its correlate, social control; and an instinctive attraction to the delegitimizing tendency, whether in the intellectual, social, or political realm.

Faced by deconstruction's unmistakable challenge to the integrity of their calling, academics not only failed to defend themselves, but also shirked their clear responsibility as scholars: that is, to report fully on the true nature of the phenomenon set before them. Instead their responses ranged from ignorance to credulity, reflecting either innocent self-deception or submissiveness in the face of intimidation—or a bit of each. In retrospect it appears that the peculiar aura of distinguished difficulty and intellectual superiority surrounding deconstruction functioned in a positively intimidating manner. Just as at present "no one *dares* to utter a liberal doctrine" when literary theory is discussed, so from the beginning observers retreated in the face of what Michel Foucault has revealingly called the "*obscurantisme terroriste*" of Derrida's prose style. One understands Foucault to be referring to the fact that any straightforward remark about Derrida's work, or about deconstruction in general—let alone a remark critical of either—is certain to be greeted with the most powerful weapon in the academic arsenal: intellectual contempt. This contempt, moreover, is always likely to be compounded with the ever ready charge of political reaction.

Both of these techniques of intimidation were used against E. D. Hirsch, whose literary theory amounted to asserting that it is possible to arrive at a close approximation of an author's intended meaning. One critic called this assertion "the intellectual equivalent of aggressiveness and a wish to dominate" and branded it as "part of an ideology of society that is authoritarian and hierarchical." Terry Eagleton called Hirsch "authoritarian and juridical" and added, predictably enough, that "the aim of all this policing is the protection of private property."

Just how much support Hirsch received from his non-deconstructionist colleagues can be surmised from the following remark by the deconstructionist Frank Lentricchia, in his book *After the New Criticism* (1980): "As a theorist who speaks unapologetically for rational values, E. D. Hirsch stands pretty much by himself in the landscape of contemporary theory." No more devastating reflection on the academic response to deconstruction could be made.

The supine intellectual posture of the academics will be familiar to anyone who recalls the variety of capitulations with which they had greeted the student movement out of which deconstruction grew. In the face of that assault, professors had swiftly abandoned their central pedagogical and scholarly convictions. They conceded that authority was by its nature coercive and that subjective impressions were as valuable as reasoned analysis. Once the countercultural assault had receded, the professors restored the status quo ante. They dropped the experimental courses they had begun to offer, returned to the traditional curriculum, and once again found reasons to demand academic work in exchange for academic grades. But capitulations have their consequences. The edifice had been shaken, and few were any longer confident about the solidarity of its underpinnings.

At present desconstruction, a product of the second, professorial wave of the student movement, promises to recede from importance in its turn. But if deconstruction failed to dislodge society's sense of reality, it was only because that sense proved to be ineradicably engrained in human nature. Once again the academics responsible for standards in their profession have been little more than bystanders as developments ran their own course. The Marxists undoubtedly have a point when they attribute the failure of deconstruction in part to its having been institutionalized by the academy, for it is true that deconstructionists have been published, favorably reviewed, tenured, and promoted—all in an academic spirit of bland receptivity that has had the ironic effect of softening the movement's impact. It is hard, though, to take encouragement from the Marxist critic who attacked Gerald Graff's *Literature against Itself* by expressing his dismay at a "growing reactionary movement in the academy to recover the ideals of logic, reason, and determinate meaning and to repudiate the radicalism of the sixties and early seventies." No such movement has ever developed.

Partisan Review, no. 2, 1986

FEMINIST

LITERARY

CRITICISM

*The greatest writers lay no stress upon
sex one way or the other. The critic is not
reminded as he reads them that he
belongs to the masculine or feminine
gender.*
—Virginia Woolf

ALTHOUGH IT PRESENTS a
united front to the world, feminist criticism has long been divided
internally and is at present undergoing a particularly far-reaching
reassessment of itself. Most of its practitioners agree that a unified
theory of feminist criticism has never emerged. One prominent characteristic of the movement, in fact—seen by some as a source of
strength and by others as a distraction—is said to be its tendency to
internal disagreement over fundamental theoretical questions. Of
these questions, the most troublesome is whether or not women's
writing differs in some essential way from men's. Without such a
gender difference, say those who argue for it, there can be no serious
feminist literary criticism. But others insist that the claim for such a
difference simply does not hold up to critical scrutiny, and must
therefore be abandoned as an ideal.

The debate represents a conflict between aesthetic theory, on the
one hand, and the imperatives of the feminist movement from which
feminist criticism sprang, on the other. The feminist movement has
of course dedicated itself to the cause of women, whereas criticism is
ordinarily supposed to represent a primary allegiance to literature.
That allegiance, previously tested by political radicals in the 1930s and
the 1960s, is being questioned again by feminists, who remain divided amongst themselves on the issue. Ironically enough, those who
have put the cause of women before the cause of literature have harbored just enough residual loyalty to literary values to compromise

their usefulness to the movement. In turn the movement has tended to undermine purely literary values. Can it be that feminist criticism has served feminism badly and has allowed literary values to be badly served in turn? If so, feminist criticism's relationship to feminism stands out as a major though not often acknowledged embarrassment.

In the meantime a much-needed assessment of feminist criticism as a whole, preferably by someone outside the movement, remains unattempted. Feminists complain that their work goes largely ignored on account of what they call gender politics on the part of men, but they underestimate the degree to which they themselves discourage serious discussion when they claim to possess an order of understanding not available to male intelligence. A few nonfeminist women critics have from time to time examined one or another aspect of the movement, but none of them has attempted to survey it systematically. (Women critics who have challenged feminist criticism include Minda Rae Amiram, Zelda Austin, Joan Didion, Carol Iannone, Diana Trilling, and Joan Malory Webber.) A recent outpouring of histories and theoretical works by feminist critics, though, has made it possible to view the evolution of the movement during its short existence since its beginnings in the early 1970s and to come to some conclusions about its theoretical disputes.

This essay leaves aside the larger task of evaluating the accomplishments of feminist literary criticism. Instead, concerned as it is with the work of feminist theorists and historians, it pursues feminist critics' own concentration on literary theory, with special emphasis on what is termed "gender theory." To be sure, literary theory, though currently held in high esteem by feminists and others, should not be the ultimate test of literary criticism. First-rate practical criticism has been known to emerge from what later came to be regarded as faulty theory, and so it may one day be with feminist criticism. At present, though, literary theory so dominates feminist and other kinds of criticism as to have put the question of practical criticism at least temporarily in the background.

Whatever their positions on gender theory, feminist critics agree that it has been a source of recurrent difficulties for them. Largely on account of gender questions, the movement has undergone several changes of direction. These changes are usually described as having followed a three-stage development on the model of a Hegelian syllogism: thesis, antithesis, and synthesis. A failed Stage One is said to have been followed by an opposite, corrective Stage Two that proved equally unsatisfactory. Finally, a Stage Three laid to rest the accumulated theoretical difficulties, gender among them. Stage One, dating to the early 1970s, is described as consisting largely of protest over the traditional depiction of women in fiction. Its practitioners asserted that literature, reflecting deep-seated prejudices in the culture, had misleadingly made women out to be passive and dependent. Attempting to elevate women's status, Stage One critics took it as their task to identify and denounce such characterizations wherever they appeared in fiction.

After a time, the account continues, it began to be evident that the rooting out of negative stereotypes was having an unintended effect. The monotonous parade of passive, dependent women characters, writes Toril Moi, produced a loss of "inspirational force," especially in classrooms. In fact, "depression" was reported to be setting in over "the essentially negative reflection" of women documented by feminist stereotype hunters "in story after story." As Elaine Showalter summed up the problem, such criticism "has a tendency to naturalize women's victimization by making it the inevitable and obsessive topic, of discussion." In short, it seems fair to say that the woman-as-victim approach not only failed to elevate the image of women but degraded it.

The second stage of feminist literary criticism, also dating to the 1970s, is represented as having taken an opposite tack in response to the failure of the first one. Instead of emphasizing the negative, the second stage sought out more acceptable depictions of women in literature. These, it was hoped, would serve as models both for women readers and for contemporary women writers. But the new "role-model" approach tended to concentrate on women authors who had displayed more of a spirit of independence in their own lives than they accorded to their heroines. This amounted to a confusion, wrote Nancy K. Miller, in which critics were reading "a heroine as the clone of her author—a reductionist strategy that has passed for literary criticism on women's writing from the beginning." Miller found that feminist criticism had further narrowed its purview by a commitment to the "authentic" representation of reality. By dismissing literary fantasy and symbolism, its critics had betrayed a preference for literature considered not aesthetically but as a source of historical information about the condition of women.

In practice, taking such an approach implied an expectation that books would depict women as an oppressed group. Not surprisingly, this expectation eventually came to be judged as "excessively naive." As Toril Moi puts it, asking for women to appear as oppressed "clashes with another demand: that for the representation of female role-models in literature." Literature cannot be authentic and ideal at the same time, for, after all, "quite a few women are 'authentically' weak and unimpressive." Carol Iannone has called this dilemma the "double bind." In her 1981 Ph.D. dissertation on feminist criticism she writes: "If women writers or characters are too successful, whether materially or morally, they cannot speak for women still oppressed. But if they are failures in achieving independence, they can hardly serve as models for other women."

The critic's double bind can also be seen in the tests applied to fictional heroines in "images-of-women" criticism—the term commonly used to refer to Stages One and Two taken together. These tests have reminded K. K. Ruthven, a male critic friendly to the movement, of "the brownie point approach" to women's studies mocked by Marilyn B. Arthur:

> If Medea gets three points for asserting herself and exacting revenge from Jason [Arthur had written], then she loses one for killing her children, forfeits another for using deceit and trickery, another for relying on her grandfather to get her out of the mess, and ends up with a score of zero.

The evaluation of characters in the manner of images-of-women criticism proves, in other words, to be so exiguous that virtually no fictional invention can satisfy it. And the result of such scrutinizing of the characters of fiction, it has to be said again, whether in the form of a hunt for stereotypes or a demand for ideal behavior, is, ironically enough, to make prominent the subject of women's inferiority instead of their equality.

Rather than emphasizing this conundrum, current discussion of feminist criticism tends to attribute the failures of the first two stages to a lack of literary-critical sophistication. The early critics failed in simplemindedly favoring realism over fantasy and symbolism, or they confused the author with her fiction, or they employed crude, point-awarding assessments of fictional characters. These shortcomings are now being said to have been overcome by Stage Three criticism. Though this stage is variously described—no two authorities seem to agree on its definition—it is marked by a new sophistication, thanks to its having adopted advanced "critical theory." This term, which once simply designated theorizing about literature, has of course come to refer to the range of French-derived, poststructuralist theories of which the best known is deconstruction. Feminist critics, among others, appear to have borrowed the recherché vocabulary of poststructuralism chiefly as a handy form of certification in today's theory-ridden academy. They have assimilated the poststructuralist challenge to authority, for example, to their own attack on patriarchy. They have also extended poststructuralism's challenge to the literary canon into a call for the inclusion in the canon of more female-authored works. And in their Stage Three criticism they have employed the Lacanian concept of "absence" to rescue the concept of a female-writing difference posited by earlier gender theory.

Thanks to critical theory, then, gender difference in writing, after its many vicissitudes under the scrutiny of earlier feminist critics, has returned to favor. In fact, defined as the assumption that "gender is a crucial determinant in the production, circulation and consumption of literary discourses," gender theory has become, according to K. K. Ruthven, the "central hypothesis" of feminist criticism. Yet despite its theoretical borrowings—or perhaps because of them—Stage Three gender theory succeeds no better than its predecessors.

In some of its original forms, gender theory held, without fear of contradiction, that one's ability to produce literature, get it circulated, and have it read is influenced by sexual identity. Feminist critics tended to stress the disadvantages in being a woman, though there can be advantages as well, but this raised no controversy. The trouble came with the attempt to make a case for an essential gender difference in the act of writing. For exactly where, they were forced to ask, can gender be identified as crucial in writing? Does it manifest itself in plot? In style? In setting? It might seem to stand to reason that women writers in the Western tradition, to the extent that they draw from experience, would concentrate on domestic matters and display a special sensitivity to details of dress and interior settings. But this kind of gender identity is decidedly not what feminist critics have in mind.

For a time it appeared that style would yield the formula of gender difference. But feminist critics themselves pointed out that the sex of an author cannot be identified from literary style alone, even by professional critics, and that the same is true of plot. This crucial point alone, demonstrated as it was by objective tests that were examined and approved by respected feminist critics, rendered gender theory unworkable. In addition, some rejected the search for gender difference for purely tactical reasons. The politically radical Toril Moi, for example, writes that "the pursuit of sex difference in language," because it tends to represent women as inferior to men, "is not only a theoretical impossibility, but a political error." Still others have pointed out that the broader doctrine of difference between women and men contradicts both feminism's original denial that women are biologically restricted and the related complaint that historically they have been stereotyped as weak in body and mind.

Despite the practical and theoretical objections, some feminist critics have maintained their allegiance to gender difference in writing. One of these, Nancy K. Miller, the critic who perciply warned against confusing authors with their heroines and who concedes that there can be "no fail-safe technique by which to determine the gender of an author," nevertheless claims to have found a gender difference in plot. Her statement of method is worth attending to not only for its content but also as an example of the kind of diction some feminist critics have been drawn toward under the influence of so-called critical theory. Miller proposes "a reading that *consciously* recreates the object it describes [gender difference], attentive always to a difference—what T. S. Eliot calls 'strong local flavor' not dependent on the discovery of an exclusive alterity." Since the word *alterity* simply means difference, Miller is actually conceding that there is no real difference after all. In logical terms what she posits is a difference without a distinction. But however designated, this nonexclusive alterity clearly falls short of supplying the gender difference posited by feminist criticism.

What, then, does Miller intend by a "reading that *consciously* recreates the object it describes"? Is she not issuing a license for the critic to supply the gender differences that the author herself failed to supply? If gender difference cannot be found, in other words, let us fabricate it. In similar fashion, another feminist critic, Rachel Blau DuPlessis, evidently frustrated in her attempts to demonstrate stylistic gender difference, nevertheless posits an aesthetic of repetition and illogic as being characteristic of female prose. Then, instead of offering examples, she attempts to incorporate these features in her own prose. She writes: "But I cannot prove that only women, that women only, use this aesthetic. And this failure is actually the strongest proof of all." Elizabeth A. Meese, meanwhile, relies on illogic pure and simple: "If what I say is true, what I say is not true."

Emotionality and illogic, though, are hardly characteristic of feminist critics. On the contrary, their writing ordinarily displays features that they would term "masculinist" or "patriarchal." They do not neglect grammar, syntax, logic, or narrative organization. Their scholarship on the whole is extensively researched, logically organized, and scrupulously footnoted—not to mention that it is often supplemented by annotated bibliographies. Feminist critics, furthermore, have not only pointed out the impossibility of differentiating female from male writing but also have analyzed the theoretical inconsistencies of one feminist critical approach after another (providing most of the refutations in the present essay). Some among them nevertheless continue to insist on feminine illogic, thereby promoting another negative stereotype of women.

Such an outcome is the result not of any retreat from logical rigor but rather of a commitment to politics. It was a political allegiance to the feminist movement of the early 1970s that produced woman-as-victim criticism in the first place. And it was failure to advance the feminist cause that led to disappointment with both this and the role-model approach by the late 1970s. Subsequently, the promise of Stage Three to remedy earlier defects was predicated on its being more rather than less politically committed, which in the 1980s meant following the wider feminist movement's shift from minimizing to emphasizing the differences between the sexes. In order to understand the evolution of feminist literary criticism, therefore, it is necessary to examine the role of politics.

To begin with, politics accounts for the oddly contradictory attitude whereby those feminist critics who exposed the failures of the earlier criticism have never fully repudiated it. In fact, as Carol Thomas Neely points out, the victim and role-model approaches actually continue in existence, though this fact goes "largely unacknowledged in many of the best-known discussions of feminist criticism." The early criticism is thus at once theoretically dismissed and tolerated in practice. How such a contradiction can be maintained may be gleaned from some observations in an essay friendly to feminist criticism by Cary Nelson. This movement, Nelson writes, is one in which "both assumptions and actual practices potentially in opposition to one another have been left largely unexplored or unacknowledged": "The reasons for that silence about implicit conflicts are essentially political. . . . By appearing to be ideologically unified, the feminist movement can be more politically effective within the general culture." The chief considerations, in other words, must always be tactical because the movement is not primarily literary but political.

Feminist critics have been the first to state that feminist scholarship "candidly serves political or social ends." For example, Toril Moi, in her explicitly titled *Sexual/Textual Politics,* writes that "the principal objective of feminist criticism has always been political," and Elizabeth Meese specifies that its "motive" is "resistance in the interest of social transformation through interpretation." This subordination of literary to political considerations need not necessarily have dictated the silent toleration of discredited critical methods. But once political considerations dictated such a course, it was adhered to—thanks to an exertion of pressure, once again best described by feminists themselves.

The movement, in Sandra M. Gilbert's words, arose out of "anger and frustration at injustice" that "got italicized into shrieks." Carolyn Heilbrun has professed herself "amazed at how high a moral tone I take," and Elaine Showalter has concluded that in at least one of its modes feminist criticism is "righteous, angry and admonitory." As K. K. Ruthven observes, the "intimidatory rhetoric of radical feminism" is used to suppress certain kinds of dissent within the movement. Dale Spender, though she does not go so far as to adopt Ruthven's term "feminist terrorism," does seem to illustrate through her own experience what Toril Moi describes as "suppression of debate within the camp." Spender reports that she suffered unpopularity simply for "declaring that feminism has no greater monopoly on truth than does patriarchy."

A similar coercion has been directed outside the movement to achieve similar ends. "Our male colleagues," writes Sandra M. Gilbert, "are increasingly reluctant" to express hostility. Despite this notable reluctance, feminist critics sometimes depict their movement as a beleaguered one. In attempting to depict feminist criticism this way, Annette Kolodny is able to cite no more than a passing unfavorable remark by Harold Bloom and a review by Robert Boyers of a book of feminist film criticism. After the appearance of Boyers's review, which Elaine Showalter joined in complaining about (for being "belligerent"), the author of the book threatened *Partisan Review* with a lawsuit, and the magazine printed a disclaimer in a subsequent issue. Criticism, let alone hostility from a male critic, was not taken kindly in this instance, nor did it go unpunished.

Jean Bethke Elshtain, writing in the magazine *Salmagundi,* has offered a subtle analysis of how feminist literary thought can result in coercion. Feminism's "sexual manicheanism"—that is, its "universal presumptions of victim/victimizer; innocent/guilty; pure/tainted"—gives rise to a hectoring style of argument. As Elshtain explains, "In order to sustain the mask of purity, the feelings of victimization, [feminist] rhetoric must bear a heavier and heavier burden of rage." Eventually, the criticism no longer represents a genuine cry of protest against victimization. Instead, the "mask of purity" assumed by feminist critics "offers a license to evade the ways in which definitions of 'victimization' are also means to coerce or control."

Coercion requires not only closing ranks to protect admittedly faulty theory like images-of-women criticism, but also passing muster as a feminist. In the introduction to *The New Feminist Criticism,* Elaine Showalter endorses Rosalind Coward's requirement that, in order to be judged feminist, books written by women should display a "shared commitment to certain political aims and objectives." Coward added that "reading a novel can be a political activity" in which books are "interrogated" to determine their true commitment to feminism.

But this is not all. It is possible for a woman critic to be rejected even if she passes the initial test. Her writing may still prove to be "an example of patriarchal aggression." The "only" way to "analyse the difference between feminist and sexist" criticism, therefore, is through "a political definition." In practice this has led to a hunt within the ranks for covertly sexist thinking. Annette Kolodny explains the technique of interrogation: Whenever a question of aesthetic judgment is at issue, the feminist asks the question "What ends do these judgments serve and what conceptions of the world or ideological stances do they (even if unwittingly) help to perpetuate?" It follows that one can trust neither a critic's female identity, nor her

use of an accepted technique of feminist criticism, nor even her professed feminism when assessing her usefulness to the movement:
politics is all.

Once loyalty and orthodoxy replace the ordinary norms of intellectual discourse, those who enforce the most Draconian standards
tend to prevail. Not even the most orthodox themselves, even those
who specialize in anathematizing other feminist critics, can feel safe.
Thus, Toril Moi finds Annette Kolodny herself guilty of unwittingly
serving the enemy. Kolodny is said to arouse suspicion by her "use of
the somewhat masculinist-sounding adjectives 'vigorous' and 'rigor-
ous,'" while her apparent belief in objective principles of literary
analysis "betrays the traditionalism" of her thinking ("traditionalism" here serving as a synonym for "masculinist"). Moi finds that another critic, Patricia Beer, though she proclaims herself interested in
"the cause of female emancipation," unacceptably adopts the ideal of
"'value-free' scholarship that feminists denounce as always subser-
vient to existing hierarchies and power structures." For Beer's devia-
tionism she is read out of the movement entirely: "If feminist criticism is a political criticism, sustained by a commitment to combat all
forms of patriarchy and sexism, Patricia Beer's book [*Reader, I Mar-
ried Him*] is evidently not a work of feminist criticism." A third critic
with apparently impeccable feminist credentials, Myra Jehlen, is
allowed by Moi to remain within the fold, but "her acceptance of the
most traditional patriarchal aesthetic categories" is called "little short
of astonishing in a critic who calls herself a feminist."

Yet not even the abandonment of aesthetic value in the service of a
revolutionary political paradigm can satisfy the most demandingly
radical of feminist critics. For them it is necessary also to abandon
the humanistic tradition from which aesthetic value has sprung. "We
had believed, I guess," writes Susan Gubar, "that women and men
participate equally in a noble republic of the spirit and that both
sexes are equal inheritors of 'a thousand years of Western culture.'"
Now she knows better. "The treasures of Western culture" prove to
be nothing more than "the patrimony of male writers." In the same
spirit, Elaine Showalter, whose credentials would seem unassailable,
has been criticized as one of those who "fail to grasp . . . that the
traditional humanism they represent is in effect part of patriarchal
ideology." Showalter has since moved to correct the impression of
tolerating humanism by identifying the common "enemies" of all

"feminist, black, and poststructuralist critics, both male and female"—namely those who "urge a return to the 'basics' and the 'classics.'"

In the final reckoning, however, Showalter, too, can always be faulted for adopting patriarchal, humanist imperatives inappropriate to feminist criticism. The very use of logic, for those who champion women's use of irrational thought and emotional prose, can qualify as a betrayal. So can "preoccupation with plot," something objected to by Mary Jacobus in her review of Sandra M. Gilbert and Susan Gubar's study of nineteenth-century women's fiction, *The Madwoman in the Attic*. What the authors of that book are said to have forgotten is that "if culture, writing, and language are inherently repressive, as they may be argued to be, so is interpretation itself." But if interpretation is oppressive, then it follows that there can be no feminist literary criticism—an unacceptable conclusion toward which radical feminists are nevertheless propelled.

Such are the results of what might be termed sexual politicization—that is, the bending of critical categories and arguments according to the needs of the feminist movement. The remaining theoretical difficulties of feminist criticism arise from what would have to be termed *political* politicization: the bending of criticism in the interest of radicalism. Historians of feminist criticism are in agreement that its range of opinion extends no further than the distance from "liberal" to "radical" to "socialist"—a description recalling the socially conscious butler in the Noel Coward play whose mistress proudly remarks that he reads everything "from the *New Statesman* to the *Daily Worker*." Elaine Showalter has stated that feminist criticism's closest "theoretical affiliations" are with "Marxist sociology and aesthetics." But, even putting Marxism aside, Left radical politics have influenced American feminist criticism at least as much as purely sexual politics. And paradoxically enough, radicalism's influence has also pushed feminist criticism in the direction of demoting instead of elevating women.

K. K. Ruthven, writing from an English point of view, traces these affiliations as follows: "Feminist criticism got under way after turning to marxism to learn how to mobilise an oppositional discourse. It has applied what it learnt so well that it is regarded by marxists as an exemplary instance of revolutionary intervention." Ruthven's emphasis on Marxism may reflect what Showalter describes as a "closer link in Britain between socialism or Marxism and feminism." But as she also points out, if American criticism started out being less explicitly Marxist than the English form, it has been increasingly influenced by European "radical critical thought" since the mid-1970s.

Radicals have taken the lead, for example, in depicting women writers as victims on account of their exclusion from the literary canon of recognized great works. Accepting this account, other feminist critics have joined them in calling for the inclusion of more women writers in anthologies and on college reading lists. Yet until recently the literary achievements of women were not ordinarily connected with femaleness. Nor did women themselves ordinarily take their sex into account. Thus when Helen Gardner removed nineteen of twenty-three women from her edition of the *Oxford Book of English Verse* in 1972, she was obviously unaware of any issue but that of critical judgment—until she was attacked. (Germaine Greer, objecting to a proposed lowering of standards in women's behalf, praised Gardner's decision). Inasmuch as women's writing began to appear extensively in print only about two hundred years ago, feminist critics, in common with Helen Gardner, have been faced with the issue of quality. In particular, should they call for the inclusion of the sentimental novels by women that dominated popular literature in the nineteenth century and that made up the bulk of early women's writing? Like literature in any popular genre, most sentimental novels were of inferior quality, as George Eliot (who tends not to be a favorite in feminist criticism) pointed out in her devastatingly witty critique, "Silly Novels by Lady Novelists."

In recognition of the problem, feminists initially treated the nineteenth-century sentimental novel as a sociological phenomenon, being careful to make no claims for its literary worth. But this necessitated calling for the introduction of second-rate writing by women into the literary canon as an act of "affirmative action," creating an impression of women's inferiority once again. Seeking to avoid this trap, the political radical falls into a worse one of repudiating literary values altogether. For radical critics assert that aesthetic standards are themselves a politically inspired imposition in the service of "interests." The privileged classes impose standards in order to install in the canon literary works calculated to help maintain the political and social status quo. Translated into feminist terms, the interests thus served are those of male literary critics acting to sustain patriarchy.

Crude as it is, the radical argument contains a grain of truth, inasmuch as any standards must to a certain extent be a reflection of the minds that constructed them. If one sets aside the Marxists' conspiratorial notions of class and privilege, it is still possible to observe the cultural limitations of literary standards (which can, in turn, still be defended as objective on balance). This is exactly how politically liberal feminist critics attempted to proceed. Nina Baym, for example, argued persuasively that the canon of American literature came to be accepted over the years partly out of extra-aesthetic considerations. Yet Baym could not bring herself to propose adding women's works to that canon on any but aesthetic grounds. Inevitably, a politically activist feminist critic, Myra Jehlen—still unrepentantly patriarchal in her application of logic—criticized Baym for "having it both ways, admitting the artistic limitations of women's fiction . . . and at the same time denying the validity of the rulers that measure these limitations." For thoroughgoing feminist political radicals, such agonizing over and finally clinging to literary value was no longer acceptable. For "to put it bluntly," as Annette Kolodny wrote, "we have had enough pronouncements of aesthetic valuation for a time."

Under just what circumstances aesthetic value will be allowed to return is not made clear. In the meantime, Ellen Carol DuBois and the other authors of *Feminist Scholarship* explain that the proper approach to the sentimental novel "involves replacing the usual standards of 'excellence' with values that examine the extent to which a work reflects or serves the interests of women." In the spirit of this directive, Jane Tompkins, repudiating the ambiguities and downright aesthetic dismissals of sentimental novels by previous feminist critics like Nina Baym, has recently offered a defense of *Uncle Tom's Cabin* as a sentimental novel. Also calling in question the concept of "excellence" by placing it in quotation marks, Tompkins asks her reader to

> set aside some familiar categories for evaluating fiction—stylistic intricacy, psychological subtlety, epistemological complexity—and to see the sentimental novel, not as an artifice of

eternity answerable to certain formal criteria and to certain psychological and philosophical concerns, but as a political enterprise, halfway between sermon and social theory.

The enterprise of *Uncle Tom's Cabin,* for Tompkins, is a women's revolution directed at the overthrow of patriarchal society. By her own insistence, the matter has become political rather than literary.

What starts out as sexual politics in feminist literary criticism, then— placing a concern to elevate women's condition before literary considerations—yields to radical politics, in which women's condition is glossed on a vaguely Marxist model of oppression and exploitation. At each radicalizing step, surprisingly enough, radical politics puts at least as much emphasis on gender as sexual politics did, advancing with equal if not greater insistence the ideas of a separate women's sensibility, a separate women's writing style, and a separate women's literary criticism. Moreover, where sexual politics had demanded ever more Draconian denials of specific literary values, radical politics demands the abandonment of literary value altogether. Where sexual politics resulted in a second-class status for women in literature, radical politics effectively fixes their status altogether beneath the level of literature. Radical politicization, in other words, escalates the demotion of women as writers and critics, and then treats apostasy with even greater severity than had merely sexual politics.

When sexual and radical politics come together, feminist critics can set upon one another with ferocity. For example, from a sexual and radical point of view not yet mentioned, the radical feminist critics so far discussed have themselves been accused of positive complicity in the oppression of women. To the lesbian feminist literary critic, they are all simply part of the "heterosexist academy." When lesbian-political tests are applied, it is seen that "heterosexist assumptions abound in literary texts, such as feminist literary anthologies, that purport to be open-minded about lesbianism." Not surprisingly, therefore, "one strain in lesbian feminist criticism" is dedicated to "unmasking" feminist criticism for the way that it ignores lesbians. As it does so, it finds that "some of the books that develop the idea of female tradition are openly homophobic, employing the word 'lesbian' only pejoratively."

Here, then, is another resentful group of female literary critics with sexually and politically determined objections—this time directed at the prejudices of feminist criticism itself, whose fundamental assumptions its members regard as sexist. Feminist criticism had held that oppressive constructs such as the traditional canon of literature and the aesthetic values that support it derived from the peculiar characteristics of men and their system of patriarchy. According to lesbian feminist theory, the same proclivity for erecting oppressive structures can be observed among feminist literary critics (as well as "contemporary feminist fiction," which, "by perpetuating stereotyped characters and themes . . . serves to 'disempower the lesbian'").

Feminist literary critics, like the male academics reluctant to express hostility to *them,* have responded to the lesbian attack with embarrassment, apologies, and tokenism. Lesbians are included but often segregated at feminist conferences and in anthologies. They have been shown acquiescence but not granted the radical reordering of literary sensibility they demand. Not that such a reordering would end the matter. For feminist critics, including even those taking a lesbian stance, would remain vulnerable to the complaints of yet another group of feminist women in literature: black feminist critics.

These critics, too, are "enraged," inasmuch as "books by black women" have been "misunderstood" and thereby "destroyed" by feminist critics. Some black critics have gone beyond the feminist rejection of white male discourse to the rejection of feminist discourse itself on the grounds that critical categories based on analyses of white women characters are Euro-American in derivation. Black feminists believe that they have suffered as well from "the racism of white lesbian feminist theory," a complaint in which they are joined by black lesbian feminist critics. The feminist critics who have been attacked, once again resembling male critics, have offered only the feeblest of responses to these charges. It is hardly sufficient for Elizabeth A. Meese to confess "my complicity as a white academic feminist," for example, or for Gayatri Chakravorty Spivak to write defensively that "the effort to put First World lesbianism in its place is not necessarily reducible to pride in female heterosexuality."

Gayatri Chakravorty Spivak's uneasiness suggests that, to be safe from recrimination, a feminist critic at the present moment would need to have not only Third World credentials like her own (or credentials as a black or "Chicana" woman), but also be a lesbian, and preferably a Marxist or at least a *soi-disant* radical at the same time. Ordinary feminist literary critics can too easily be assailed as hetero-sexist, homophobic, racist, or guilty of "cultural imperialism." On the other hand, lesbian and black critics have found their own respective schools theoretically inadequate. Each started out by attempting to define unique characteristics by which a lesbian or black lesbian author's writing might be distinguished. But female heterosexual writers sometimes also fit the attempted definitions—along with certain male writers—while certain lesbian writers did not. With black lesbian writing, not only did certain heterosexual black female writers fit the attempted definitions, but "there are probably a few Black male writers who qualify as well."

The sexually and politically ideal writer, it can be concluded, like the ideal critic, can never be found. Yet although in the end the fate of race difference in writing has been the same as that of gender difference—refutation by feminists themselves—demands for sexual and political purity have kept rising. And the more radical the politics, the greater has been the need to assert a biological difference of one or another kind. Once again ignoring the case against female difference in writing style, the most radical feminist critics have argued that women writers and readers differ from men not only in that they prefer to be less logical, but also because they are intrinsically less coherent intellectually. The gender difference that produces this result, they assert, derives from women's speech. Unlike men, the argument goes, women speak without purpose. They "chatter," going "off in all directions." They vaguely assign sentimentalized values to people and things, as in their unique use of the words *sweet* and *divine* as unironic terms of praise. In a corresponding manner, women's writing, according to radical critics, programmatically neglects grammar, syntax, logic, and narrative organization.

Appropriately, it has fallen to the French, who have developed the most politically radical tendencies in feminist criticism, to make the most intransigent theoretical case for the proposition that women are weak-willed and weak-minded. Women's chemical and physical makeup, explains Luce Irigaray, a prominent French theorist, renders them "temperamental, incomprehensible, perturbed, capricious." Women writers, the French critic Julia Kristeva asserts, for these reasons function primarily as "hysterics," and their prose should be traced to "the predominance in them of drives related to anality and childbirth." Under the influence of poststructuralism, these critics have managed to arrive at the paradoxically reductive assumptions of what Toril Moi characterizes as "clear biologism"—the proposition that women's biological makeup dictates how they think, read, and write. Not hesitating to follow the biological imperative all the way, they have arrived at yet another characterization of women virtually identical with the hoariest of stereotypes.

Drawing on a second notion from Jacques Lacan—his characterization of the phallus as "the primary signifier"—French criticism does not hesitate, either, to ask the logical question (in the words of Sandra M. Gilbert and Susan Gubar): "If the pen is a metaphorical penis, from what organ can females generate texts?" The reply—that it must be the female genitalia—appears evident enough and has been widely accepted. (Hélène Cixous, it is true, employs an alternate "Kleinian analysis of the mother's nipple as a pre-Oedipal penis image," but she has been faulted for a superficial willingness to "happily integrate both penis and nipple.") Still, once the female genitalia are agreed upon, just which part should be "privileged"? At this point in the argument, the escalation of terms continues in a most baroque fashion. For on the hermetic battleground of the female genitalia, too, are to be found a political Left and Right, patriarchy, imperfect feminism, and finally an ideal radical stance based on the one correct attitude towards the parts of the anatomical structure in question.

Luce Irigaray champions the vulva. In her theoretical system the unique experience of pleasure derived from the labia, "two lips which embrace each other continuously," is the basis of the self-indulgent, illogical thinking and writing—*"jouissance"*—that should and will become characteristic of women. K. K. Ruthven has pointed out that uncircumcised men can be said to experience in their foreskins comparable self-stimulation to the two lips of the vulva, but this theoretical objection has apparently not yet been dealt with.

An American, Naomi Schor, holds that Irigaray tends "'to valorize the vagina' at the expense of the clitoris"—an evidently more weighty objection. Schor seems to be suggesting that such "valorization" falls into the patriarchal habit of delegitimizing the clitoris—something radical feminists have taxed other feminists with in the past. Schor calls on feminist critics to correct the shortcomings of Irigaray's approach by developing a "clitoral hermeneutics." But here radical politics proves to be at odds with itself. For even before such a project can be completed, a political objection has already been raised by other feminists—namely that *jouissance*, whether it be clitorally or labially derived, excludes Third World women who have undergone clitoridectomies. Irigaray's vaginal criticism, in any case, like other feminist theories before it, has been dismissed as "completely under the influence of patriarchal ideology."

To be sure, some feminist critics have not failed to remark on the paradox of confirming the very stereotype of women as weak-willed and weak-minded that the movement began by denouncing. They warn that the French or any other model of illogical female thought and writing leads toward a return to patriarchy. Raising such an objection, though, risks the appearance of naivete. One must display an awareness that the allusive, punning style in which French radical feminists, elaborately and with exaggeration, advance the stereotype of the illogical woman is intended partly as a "transvaluing" of the stereotype—a reversal, rather than a confirmation, of its implications.

[Taking their cue from the French, some feminist literary critics have gravitated toward making puns, usually based on literary terms. Male thinking is the most frequent target, though the puns may be derived from male authors. The expressions include "phallacy," "Phallocracy," and "phallogocentrism" (from Derrida). One understands that "manglish" and "hismeneutics" are to be replaced, for the previously "immasculated" female reader, by "sisspeak" and "sapphistry"—or more vulgarly, by the "*con*centric," by "con-texte," and by "Gyn/Ecology" (italics in original).]

The French, furthermore, do not exactly claim that women's writing is at present an expression of the female body: their biologic formulation is advanced only as a prospective and utopian construct. Other feminists have nevertheless perceived a danger in positing the biological determinism of women's writing. Yet having done so, they stop short of dissociating themselves from the French. Once again, it appears, the demands of solidarity, this time thanks to the powerful lesbian, poststructuralist, and politically radical credentials of French feminism, have triumphed over literary judgment.

It may well be asked how the spirit of feminist solidarity differs from the tolerance normally extended by literary criticism to a range of opposing viewpoints. For that matter, what is the objection to bias itself, inasmuch as it has always been an accompaniment of literary criticism (in common with other kinds of investigation)? The answer is that there is a crucial distinction between intended and unintended bias—between being inadvertently influenced by politics and choosing subordination to its aims and principles. Feminist critics elevate a deficit into a principle when, observing breaches of objectivity in others, they adopt the same failing in the service of their cause.

What has been forgotten is that the value of the literary critical enterprise does not lie in its ability to perform any direct services to society. On the contrary, for the most part criticism operates within an enclosure, and in this space the highest value is aesthetic. By the measure of social needs, the aesthetic would have to be rated low on the scale of values, yet in literature it represents the equivalent of morality. In a similar way, literary criticism substitutes for the pursuit of truth the pursuit of a satisfactory account of the aesthetic object. Literary criticism may never achieve a perfect account, but in attempting to reach one it imitates moral action. The absence of such an attempt is what makes it appear to us that something is amiss when a critic consciously adopts a bias—just as we are disturbed by cheating at cards. In both situations we sense analogies with actual social morality.

Feminist critics, though, have repudiated the morality of the aesthetic. Seizing on the poststructuralist argument that we can never achieve objectivity, or on the Marxist argument that all taste reflects social conditioning, they have justified their subordination of literary values to the needs of the women's movement, or of radical politics, or both. Until and unless feminist criticism commits itself to aesthetic value, one can predict, it will continue to turn in on itself, repudiating one stage after another of necessarily inadequate theory.

In view of the internal pressures against such a change of heart within feminist criticism, it may seem churlish to quarrel with those few American feminists who have been intrepid enough to challenge the biological extremism of radical French feminism. Yet when couched as a warning against the danger of a return to "patriarchy," this defense of women's dignity prompts the question of whether traditional society ever really went so far in denigrating women as feminist criticism itself has gone. In the past, surely, stereotypes of the sexes were understood as tendencies, not absolutes. When men and women were stigmatized, it was typically because of their occasional, not their immutable, vulnerabilities. In feminist criticism, by contrast, women have come to be defined almost exclusively by their putative limitations.

Striking as the failure of feminist criticism is, with its seemingly fatal tendency to denigrate rather than elevate women, it is not the first literary movement to have suffered from its own theory. A comparably tortuous path of self-contradiction can be traced in the development of Marxist criticism in this century. In fact, Marxist criticism preceded the reversals of feminist criticism when it moved from the espousal of (socialist) realism to an embrace of its opposite in the deconstructive assault on reality. With Marxist and feminist criticism alike, the tergiversations and self-contradictions, the mutually recriminatory denunciations for straying from orthodoxy stem not from incompetence but from the primacy of politics.

It is not surprising, therefore, that the extremes of critical self-contradiction in feminist criticism tend to correlate with extreme politicization, as in the case of the French feminists, most of whom are declared Marxists. But what of liberal as opposed to radical criticism? In common with other movements, feminism deserves to be judged by how the representatives of its central tendency deal with the challenges of extremists. From this point of view, it has to be said that when it comes to French structuralist biologism, to Marxism, white and black lesbianism, and other radical forms of expression, mainstream liberal feminist criticism has allowed itself to be taken intellectually hostage. By subordinating literary critical values to considerations of political solidarity and a desire not to insult political radicals, it has made itself complicit in radical feminism's most damaging tendencies.

The final question to be asked is what effect the emergence of feminist literary criticism will have on literature and literary criticism in the long run. It may well be that, thanks to its unsupportable claims to a unique aesthetic and a separate language, feminist criticism will remain a largely isolated phenomenon. On the other hand, its implication that women have played minor roles as writers and incompetent ones as critics seem destined to hang in the air for some time to come. By positing the theory of a separate, yet-to-be-recognized women's tradition of writing, feminist criticism has had and will continue to have the effect of excluding women from literature—and not only from literature. For, by asserting that language is for women "something like a foreign tongue," feminist criticism denies them their role in the development of human speech. From yet another point of view, feminist criticism cannot logically credit women with a significant role in any other phase of human cultural development because, if it did, then the conclusion might follow that "gender identity and ideologies of gender" were "created by women as well as men" (something Marxist feminists do allow). In all of these ways feminist literary criticism surrenders to men the characteristics and habits of mind by which the progress of civilization has always been driven. The world's scientific and cultural progress to date is in effect attributed to men and mankind's future prospects assigned to their exclusive care.

The one broad avenue to participation in the life of the culture always thought to have been open to women—literature's noble republic of the spirit—is in one way or another effectively denied women by feminist criticism. Yet it was through literature that Mary Ann Evans, writing as George Eliot, could confront her world unfettered by any limitations that might be thought to attach to her as a woman. Through literature Emily Dickinson and Willa Cather were free to write poems and stories in which the "I" who speaks is male rather than female, thereby claiming their privilege to speak for any kind of human being their imaginations were capable of grasping. Feminist critics, in contrast, would in the name of liberation circumscribe women's participation in literature in exactly the fashion that they imagine women to have been circumscribed by society. In the determinedly enlightened atmosphere of our present literary culture, it hardly seems possible that a movement whose effect is thus to denigrate women could be tolerated. Yet in a field where women's excellence is incontestable, feminist literary critics, starting out in the conviction that women writers had long suffered at the hands of male critics, have ended up fostering an image of women at least as insulting as any that they set out to protest.

The American Scholar, Autumn 1988

NOTE: Among the books surveyed for this essay were the following: *Crossing the Double-Cross: The Practice of Feminist Criticism,* by Elizabeth A. Meese (University of North Carolina Press, 1986); *Feminist Criticism and Social Change: Sex, Class and Race in Literature and Cul-*

ture, ed. Judith Newton and Deborah Rosenfelt (Methuen, 1985); *Feminist Literary Studies: An Introduction,* by K. K. Ruthven (Cambridge University Press, 1984); *Feminist Scholarship: Kindling in the Groves of Academe,* jointly written by Ellen Carol DuBois, Gail Paradise Kelly, Elizabeth Lapovsky Kennedy, Carolyn W. Korsmeyer, and Lillian S. Robinson (University of Illinois Press, 1985); *For Alma Mater: Theory and Practice in Feminist Scholarship,* ed. Paula Treichler, Cheris Kramarae, and Beth Stafford (University of Illinois Press, 1985); *Gender and Reading: Essays on Readers, Texts, and Contexts,* ed. Elizabeth A. Flynn and Patrocinio P. Schweickart (Johns Hopkins University Press, 1986); *The New Feminist Criticism: Essays on Women, Literature and Theory,* ed. Elaine Showalter (Pantheon Books, 1985); *Sexual/Textual Politics: Feminist Literary Theory* by Toril Moi (Methuen, 1985).

AMERICAN
LITERATURE

LITERARY
SCHOLARSHIP
AND DISPARAGING
AMERICAN
CULTURE

SINCE THE 1960s critics have re-
placed the themes of innocence and achievement traditionally found
in American literature with an opposite emphasis on guilt and failure. The dark side of the national imagination is of course no new
discovery. Previous interpreters had not neglected James Fenimore
Cooper's regrets over American treatment of the Indians, or Hawthorne's rehearsals of old crimes committed against the Quaker mi-
nority, or Herman Melville's pointed finger of accusation at Americans for their racial crimes. The same interpreters, though, tended to
find a vision of perfection alongside the guilt and alienation in American literature—and to associate this vision just as firmly with America as any of its crimes.

It was in America or at least as the result of America's existence,
after all, that Melville and Mark Twain projected ideal bondings between men of opposite races, and it was in terms of America's future
that Hawthorne could imagine the emancipation of women. For
critics of the present time, however, the American democratic experiment evoked by such visions has come to be regarded as something
suitable for discussion strictly in terms of its shortcomings.

On the other hand those who evidently feel this way do not declare themselves in so many words. Instead of explicitly attacking American culture or devaluing American literature, they tend to inflate the importance of minor works and works about minorities. The new view has been conveyed, then, through an unspoken political indictment. One drops certain remarks friendly to a radical critique of America. The critic's own politics are presumably milder than the sympathies he thus conveys, but it is the latter for which he would like to take credit. So common has this kind of signaling become and so well does it express current academic attitudes that reviewers have hardly found it worthy of comment.

For precisely the reason that post-1960s criticism of American literature has been neither explicit nor publicly recognized, it appears worthwhile to bring its assumptions into the light of day. A number of recent works offer a good opportunity to do this. Each of them offers itself for comparison with past criticism by taking up what has probably been the central concern of American literary scholarship from the beginning: the fate of the democratic idea.

Democracy emerged as the central theme of American literary criticism around the turn of this century. At that time of the first attempts to view American literature as a distinct entity, critics focused on a long history of pronouncements on democracy by American writers. They found that early writers and critics alike had called for a democratic literary revolution comparable to the American political revolution.

At the beginning of the 1920s, when D. H. Lawrence defined what has since been accepted as "classic" American literature, he linked together the nineteenth century's disparate works by finding in them a common impulse to break away from the worn-out forms of Europe. Ultimately this impulse was democratic. Not long afterward, in extending Lawrence's paradigm, V. L. Parrington and F. O. Matthiessen came to regard American literature as involving an ever-broadening inclusion of the common people—a process roughly representing these critics' conception of the democratic idea.

In the early 1970s, a few years after 1960s culture had made its full impact, a new attitude toward American democratic myths began to reach print. Where before skeptical but tolerant indulgence had been typical, now blanket distrust became the norm. The transition to this view can be traced in the works of certain critics who wrote both before and after the 1960s. The most important of these was Henry

Nash Smith. In 1950 he published what is still the definitive study of the myth of the American West. In *Virgin Land: The American West as Symbol and Myth,* Smith explored the ramifications in literature and history of what he called "the myth of the garden"—a belief in the American West as a fount of both natural goodness and democracy. Smith pointed out the artistic and political limitations of such an idealized view. But for him the myth's hold over men's imaginations represented an essential part of the experience of the nineteenth century. And if the myth of the garden proved to be "erroneous," it was nevertheless true to experience. The myth accurately expressed "beliefs and aspirations as well as statistics."

In 1974 Smith undertook to review a book whose thesis clashed with his own. This was Richard Slotkin's *Regeneration through Violence: The Mythology of the American Frontier, 1600–1860.* Slotkin posited a very different myth of the western frontier: a dream based on the violence committed by whites against Indians. The reimagination of that violence, Slotkin argued, acted as a psychically regenerative ritual—one that served to overcome the inner insecurities of Americans. Regeneration had been one of Smith's own themes. The western land, he had written, was at one time expected to bring about a "regeneration, a rejuvenation of man and society." Without ignoring frontier violence, Smith treated it as something that had been struggled *against* in the literature, not as the very basis of the myth of the West.

In his review Smith found that Slotkin had not supported his thesis. Yet Smith feared that his own scholarly standards might have produced an incapability of "doing justice to Slotkin, who represents a younger generation that values intuition and imagination more highly than precise definition and traditional procedures of verification." Putting aside his cranky old notions of verification, then, Smith pronounced the closing words of Slotkin's book "a moving and persuasive piece of rhetoric." The passage in question contrasted sharply with *Virgin Land'*s picture of a hopeful if flawed nation. For now America was become the country of "the Indian debased, impoverished, and killed in return for his gifts; the land and its people, its 'dark' people especially, economically exploited and wasted . . . the piles of wrecked and rusted cars, heaped like Tartar pyramids of death-cracked, weather-browned, rain-rotted skulls, to signify our passage through the land."

Four years after reviewing Slotkin, Smith adopted a similarly disillusioned view of American popular culture in *Democracy and the Novel: Popular Resistance to Classic American Authors* (1978). Smith explained that he retained his interest in "the secular faith or ideology lying at the base of American popular culture." But instead of continuing to explore the positive literary uses of this faith, he now wished to detail the ways in which it hampered and even crippled American writers.

His subtitle indicated that popular culture, instead of sustaining the American imagination, offered "popular *resistance*" to classical American writers. As for the myth of America itself—here described as belief "that the United States was the last best hope of humanity: the repository of freedom, the standard-bearer of progress, the land of opportunity"—this was now seen as little more than the expression of a debased bourgeois taste. The fate of the word *democracy* in *Democracy and the Novel* was to be identified with a scorned middle class and to be equated with bad taste in literature.

Larzer Ziff's *Literary Democracy: The Declaration of Cultural Independence in America* (1981) is a new work on the classic period of American writing in the nineteenth century. Unlike most studies of that period it accords extended serious treatment to a number of minor writers. Taken together, these writers give the appearance of having been included in order to certify the author's post-1960s credentials. For example Margaret Fuller, "who spoke better than she wrote" and "was far more commanding in person than on the page," receives an entire chapter—apparently for her feminism. The "modest literary powers" of Harriet Beecher Stowe, also treated at chapter length, bring in the race issue. And in a chapter on George Washington Harris, "who has not written more than ten consecutive pages that can be read without wincing," Ziff praises that author for capturing all that is admirable in the spirit of the southern folk: "antiintellectualism, sexual vigor, anti-authoritarianism, and cruel physical force buried in the psyche."

Other odds and ends of the sensibility of the 1960s emerge when Ziff turns to the major authors of the American renaissance. Walt Whitman is elevated for having come from a "physical and social environment" that was "fleshy, turbulent, lower-class, boastful, gaudy, leering." Thoreau, who "on the surface appeared to be a laissez-faire capitalist run wild," in fact engaged in "flagrant countercultural be-havior." And Emerson, though "curiously" enough "totally dis-trustful of collective action," may be thought of as a critic of the "rav-ages" of "unrestricted capitalistic enterprise."

It is with another minor writer, George Lippard, that the contem-porary source for Ziff's analyses is almost clearly apparent. Lippard, "whose writing only occasionally rises above that of the mere hack," is accorded a chapter on the strength of his revolutionary sympa-thies. When Lippard's politics prove to include conspiracy theory, Ziff contrives to turn this circumstance to advantage. For Lippard to have been "rooted in the widespread if frequently inarticulate folk-lore of paranoia in his society" is a good thing, because Lippard's nightmares serve to "reveal the underside of America's proclaimed concept of itself."

This denial of the American myth takes in far more than the West and comes closer than either Slotkin or Henry Nash Smith to stating the central concern of post-1960's criticism. For that concern has been not so much to repudiate one or another myth of the past but rather to reject American culture itself. In Ziff's case such a rejection might seem to be at odds with the idea in his book's title. The term *literary democracy,* after all, appears to carry forward the Parrington-Matthiessen tradition of celebrating American literature for bringing the people into books and books to the people. In fact, though, de-mocracy is eventually redefined in terms suitable for the 1980s.

Ziff presents Hawthorne, for example, as having approved demo-cratic principles even when these were demagogic. Such principles, Hawthorne is said to have believed, "did arise finally from the un-tutored passions of the people rather than from calculation." This is a highly questionable proposition: most critics have found Hawthorne to be opposed to demagogy in any form. But more important than whether the proposition is right or wrong is its effect on the mean-ings of the words *democracy* and *the people*. The American people—a long-recognized protagonist in American literature—are no longer to be thought of as ordinary men and women in search of land, work, and personal freedom. The people are now represented in-stead as a dissident roiling underclass. As for democratic principles, these are no longer to be judged by their content but by their class origins. Writers, in turn, are to be assessed by their degree of friendliness to this newly defined people no matter what principles it may represent. Thus Hawthorne is praised for supposedly having been "in his fictions a vigorous defender of the mob." He is said to have in fact "used the mob as the standard of emotional health in his fictions."

Untutored passions, demagogy, the mob. Together these make democracy over into a dream of the 1960s: make it, that is to say, a radical force opposed to American culture itself. For Ziff the ultimate touchstones of democracy lie in times of disruption. He claims particular significance for the opening date of his survey, 1837, the year of a financial panic. In fact very little is said of this date after the introduction. By vaguely conjuring with it, though, Ziff presents himself as one sensitive to a failure of capitalism—something that places him on the progressive side as it is currently conceived by many academics. Similarly invoked is 1848, the year of revolutions in Europe. If this date is properly taken into account, Ziff explains, the love of country expressed by Melville in a well-known passage from *White-Jacket* need not be an embarrassment. "Let us always remember," Melville wrote, "that with ourselves, almost for the first time in the history of the earth, national selfishness is unbounded philanthropy; for we can not do a good to America but we give alms to the world." The correct way to read this passage, Ziff explains, is with a pinch of "sea salt." It will then be seen that in the wake of the 1848 revolutions Melville is really only trying to buck people up by providing "the chauvinistic fare his countrymen craved." Ziff concludes that "had not freedom seemed to have failed everywhere but in America, it would be difficult to respect Melville" for having expressed such manifestly absurd sentiments.

Eventually Ziff adds "savagery" to the mob as an essential ingredient of democracy. To do this he must attempt to make the case that *Typee,* Melville's book about his sojourn among cannibal islanders of the South Seas, is more friendly to savagism than to civilization. Stepping back from the narrator's vividly described fear of being swept up in the natives' savage practices, Ziff concludes with professorial objectivity that the narrator "can never rid himself of his fear of their reported cannibalistic practices although, in fact, he experiences only comfort at their hands." Yet no mere "report" has terrified the narrator and led him to flee his comforting hosts, but rather a view of a pot containing chunks of fresh human meat. Ziff supposes Melville to be saying that savagery "was a term applicable to the Europeans' colonial and missionary activities in the Pacific rather than to the people they practiced upon." Savagery properly understood is actually the essence of democracy, which must be sustained by our "nurturing the savage in each breast."

In Alan Trachtenberg's *The Incorporation of America: Culture and Society in the Gilded Age* (1982), the new critical spirit—disenchantment with American culture and generalized friendliness to the anticapitalist dissident spirit, even to the point of supplying it where lacking—is not so much expressed as assumed. Whereas Henry Nash Smith felt the need to reject American myths and Ziff to redefine civilization and savagery, Trachtenberg simply places terms in ironic quotation marks. Thus he can write that his first chapter deals with the West as myth—"especially 'civilization' wrested from its perceived opposite, the 'savage' cultures of Indians." Elsewhere he employs equally ironic quotation marks when using the words "progress," "art," "scientific," "culture," and—most revealing of all—"Americanization." With similar irony he also places in quotation marks "architecture," "real estate," and the word "better" in the phrase "desire for a better material life."

For Trachtenberg the entire post–Civil War period trails a series of ironies. Westward expansion amounted to "conquest, settlement, and exploitation." Not only did the Indians suffer, but the settlers had their dream and their land destroyed by "overmechanized" farming. In the East the machine was made into an object of worship. Once again ironic quotation marks serve to indicate the author's contempt—this time for those who welcomed labor-saving machinery as a "human benefactor" and a "great emancipator of man from the bondage of labor." The only bright spot in the period is provided by workers, whom Trachtenberg credits with organizing "a collectivist counterculture," and with having "tended to view wage labor as another form of slavery . . . and the monied classes as usurpers."

Trachtenberg's analysis amounts to a combination of Lewis Mumford on the ravaging of civilization by technology and versions of Karl Marx in which a society's industrial base is said to control its cultural perceptions—or more properly its *mis*conceptions. In the Mumford tradition Trachtenberg makes the apparent dynamism of America's territorial and industrial expansion part of a universal process of "incorporation." As the result of this process the entire civilization supposedly took on the undesirable characteristics of the then developing business corporation. For example, corporate standardized weights and measures were imposed despite the "infinitely complex needs" of a diverse people. The result was that "standardization of basic perceptions infiltrated the society."

In neo-Marxist terms new mechanical and cultural developments are treated as disguises that cover up exploitation and control. "Incorporation," for example, "disguised itself in continued spectacles such as Central Park." The park's well-laid-out paths, together with better lighting in the rest of the city, were really "campaigns against mystery" that helped to dull and subjugate the people. The architecture of office buildings similarly disguised the "arcane transactions" taking place within, while "the origins of goods" were disguised by department stores. Suitably accompanying these sinister developments, buried beneath city streets were "mechanical intrusions into homes: gas and water lines, plumbing, electricity." (Elsewhere, though, Trachtenberg complains of delays in bringing these same intrusive sewer lines to "the quarters of the poorest workers and recent immigrants.")

Trachtenberg's biases are made apparent from comparison with a book unaffected by the influence of the 1960s: the late Howard Mumford Jones's *The Age of Energy: Varieties of American Experience 1865–1915* (1971). Jones did not ignore systematized political corruption, dishonest machinations by speculators in the building of railroad networks and the settlement of western lands, or the evils of corporations. But he felt that the time had come to answer indictments (like Lewis Mumford's) of the Gilded Age. In the long perspective, he asserted, "the stunning record of advance in science and technology" made the years from 1865 to 1915 "a brilliant epoch." After all, despite financial depressions and corruption, the machine "lightens toil, increases comfort, creates more wealth and more science, and is a primary power for the general welfare."

Trachtenberg is unable to deny the evidences of progress that underlie this conclusion. Instead of doing so, therefore, he is vaguely dismissive on the subject. Thus, regarding estimates of the degree to which mechanical advances in the course of the nineteenth century had increased individual output (a multiplier of eighteen in the case of farm work), he contents himself with commenting darkly that "in such figures the American propensity for mechanical improvement *seemed* to bear its most impressive fruit" (italics mine).

Trachtenberg had seen things quite differently before the impact of the late 1960s. The intellectual distance between his *Brooklyn Bridge* (1965) and *The Incorporation of America* can be expressed as the distance between a pre- and a post-1960s cultural outlook. *Brooklyn Bridge* celebrated a mechanical construction symbolic of the Gilded Age. To be sure, like Henry Nash Smith in *Virgin Land*, Trachtenberg by no means started out as a mindless booster. For example, he pointed out that inasmuch as the bridge represented a final link in an east-west network of industrializing roads, it ended the Jeffersonian dream that "roads would protect the agrarian republic." Yet Trachtenberg concluded that while one might entertain a passing regret over the end of the earlier dream, "American society had to become technological in order to survive."

Trachtenberg interpreted "Passage to India," Walt Whitman's paean to industrial progress, in this light. (Actually the poem was written in the late 1860s, before completion of the bridge.) For Whitman the railroads crossing the American continent promised a "passage to India," by which he meant a trade route to Asia. In Henry Nash Smith's *Virgin Land* the dream of completing such a route was one of the ruling images, and Trachtenberg in *Brooklyn Bridge* quoted Smith on the dream as "a symbol of freedom and of national greatness." Whitman, to be sure, enforced the conventional moral that mechanical advances omit something spiritual in human life, and asserted that this something is to be supplied by the poet. If this did not go far enough, Trachtenberg felt, it was because at worst Whitman had failed to consider that the march of progress under the engineer would by its mechanical nature "very likely postpone appreciably the metaphysical passage to India."

Discussing "Passage to India" in *The Incorporation of America,* Trachtenberg attempts to find new reservations on Whitman's part in the poem itself—reservations going well beyond Trachtenberg's own previous notion of utopia postponed. "The poet seems to complete the work of the engineer," Trachtenberg now writes, and then asks: "Or does he remedy it, restoring what the machine has split asunder?" Most critics would agree that the poet does *not* express the need to "remedy" progress, much as Trachtenberg might like him to. Nor would most critics agree that the poem "seems to undercut the value of the magnificent engineering achievements by subordinating them to the work of the *poet*." On the contrary Whitman clearly restricts himself to telling the great engineers that as a poet he must consider "not your deeds *only*."

Trachtenberg, then, has sharply changed his views of the age and its literature, and presumably of the Brooklyn Bridge itself, the structure that inspired his earlier book but now gains no mention. The entire period has become for him a chronicle of "incorporation and violence," and he suggests that the words "weird and ghastly story" would make a suitable epigraph for his own account of it.

In the end Trachtenberg goes so far as to defend the discredited conspiracy theories of the nineteenth-century Populists. Howard Mumford Jones exposed the misconceptions underlying these lurid accounts of evil corporate machinations. Richard Hofstadter studied the same theories from a psychopathological point of view in *The Paranoid Style in American Politics*. Larzer Ziff, despite his literary enthusiasm for the agitated, dreamlike quality of the same conspiracy theories, at least gave them no credit in themselves. In contrast Trachtenberg concludes that when the Populists used the term *conspiracy* they "called Satan by his modern name: monopolies and corporations."

Trachtenberg's perceptive Populists and his wise and virtuous workers may have lived in the nineteenth century, but they were born in the 1930s. The latter period is the focus of Marcus Klein's *Foreigners: The Making of American Literature, 1900–1940* (1981). Looking back at the record of democratic ideas in the 1930s, Klein shows just how workers, along with "the people" and "the folk," were idealized. Himself a contributor to the Parrington-Matthiessen tradition of the literary march of democracy, though, Klein argues that through such idealization the 1930s did effect an admirable "democratization of the ideas of authorship in America."

Klein puts it that at the turn of the nineteenth century "America vanished." By this he means that at about that time an overwhelmingly nativist American population shifted to being a population of immigrants as well. The "literary right," represented by T. S. Eliot, Ezra Pound, and even F. Scott Fitzgerald, rejected the newcomers. Employing exclusivity, ethnic slurs, the invocation of tradition, and modernist obscurity, the literary right attempted to recapture its cultural hegemony. The "foreigners" nevertheless made their way into the American tradition by making literature out of their own experiences: notably those of the ghetto and poverty.

It is one thing, though, to explore the role of class and ethnic experience in literary creation and quite another to suggest, as Klein does, that the new material constituted "an aesthetic of a sustaining, even joyous, vitality in the lower depths." Klein believes that this vitality had its realization in a "relevant" literature of "plain fact." The new literature formed an "avant-garde" counter to the symbolizing avant-garde of literary modernism. Analyzing a poem by Robinson Jeffers, Klein finds in it "a nice sense of the experiential harshnesses in which wisdom and beauty have being," and he asserts that such a realization is "of the left." At this point he has fallen into the literary fallacy described by Lionel Trilling in "Reality in America": valuing harsh (presumably lower-class) reality over other experience.

In his wish to give his authors the imprimatur of a vital democratic aesthetic, Klein forgets that they themselves resisted just such definition. Henry Roth, the author of *Call It Sleep*, traced his own literary inspiration to James Joyce. Some years later Ralph Ellison rejected attempts like Klein's to posit a black ethnic aesthetic, insisting that *his* influences, too, came from reading Joyce and other literary moderns. It could well be argued that, far from erecting an alternative aesthetic, the writers of the 1930s were most successful precisely when they were most influenced by modernism.

If this should prove to be true, though, Klein's enthusiasm would still place him in a very different category from the bitter and resentful post-1960s critics. For Klein remains faithful to the central tradition of American literary criticism. He may link his aesthetic to a spirit of protest, but he treats its lower-class, ghetto, and folk roots as essential parts of the American experience. In contrast, in their determination to reject American culture, the post-1960s critics avoid treating either minorities or protest as expressions of American culture.

In this criticism literary, political, and economic failures may all be traced to the influence of American culture, but achievements in these areas are somehow never to be positively associated with that same culture. This formula of inclusion and exclusion was the basis of what Henry Nash Smith identified as a new kind of scholarship in

Richard Slotkin's *Regeneration through Violence*. The same formula is expressed in Alan Trachtenberg's use of ironic quotation marks and in Henry Nash Smith's contention in *Democracy and the Novel* that popular democratic taste injured serious literature. That which finds favor in the post-1960s intellectual universe must either be opposed to American culture or else appear as one of its casualties. Thus Smith holds up realism as an indigenous movement opposed to the values of the dominant American culture of the late nineteenth century, but tells its story in terms of defeat.

Critics have every right to adopt such views. They are free to offer a picture of the United States as a nation that committed genocide against the Indians and in the Philippines, exploited its own workers as though they were slaves, grew into an imperialist power, anticipated Hitler by the way it treated communists after the First World War, and revealed a "fascist medievalism" during the Vietnam war. (These opinions are gathered from Klein, Trachtenberg, Ziff, and *America and the Patterns of Chivalry* (1982), by John Fraser, an otherwise balanced look at conservative and radical cultural styles.) But reviewers, in turn, have a responsibility to point out what is being said, and a right to suggest that henceforth it be said less equivocally. And they have a right, too, to insist that the case against America should be presented directly, not dropped en passant as part of some other discussion. If American culture is to be rejected, the process should at least be brought into the open. That way it will no longer be so easy to present the items in the implied indictment as facts.

To social scientists and other humanists it may appear that by its nature literary criticism consists of no more than opinion. Yet, although objectivity can never be guaranteed, literary criticism is subject to at least one check on subjectivity. A scholar must take into account previous interpretations. These may not be ignored, no matter what the critic's opinion of them. Once previous interpretations are taken into account, no matter from what point of view, the clash of rival opinions is thrown open to the scrutiny of other critics, and thereby to at least theoretically possible resolution.

This is not to say that a literary scholar is bound to bog down his narrative in order to air each of his disagreements with previous authorities—only that the critic who chooses not to argue a controversial point should indicate that he is expressing his own opinion. It should not be enough for critics of American literature to run one or another cultural period through a sieve of irony whose strands are made up of post-1960s shibboleths. Only when opinions are stated clearly and facts distinguished from opinion can the evaluation of American culture be raised from the level of insinuation where it now resides.

Sewanee Review, Spring 1983

CIVILIZATION'S
MALCONTENTS:
RESPONSES TO
TYPEE

―――――――――

TYPEE, HERMAN MELVILLE'S
slightly fictionalized memoir of his stay among the cannibal islanders
of the Marquesas in 1842, was a first, youthful work. Melville went on
to write three more books about his seagoing adventures, always improving his skill as a writer. And yet none of these works—not *Omoo*
nor *Redburn* nor *White-Jacket*—comes close to recapturing the literary power and philosophical suggestiveness of *Typee*. Not only did
Typee establish Melville's fame, first in England and then in the United
States, but it continued to be read when *Moby-Dick* was forgotten,
and still occasions new interpretations, most of them having to do
with the question of Melville's allegiance to civilization.

The tale begins when an ill-managed, foul, depressing whaler sails
into the bay of a paradisal island. Two adventurous youths—Melville, who is the book's narrator, and his friend Toby—jump ship
and escape into the interior. Unexpectedly, the highlands to which
they flee turn out to be cold and forbidding. They have planned to
seek out a peaceful tribe called the Happars, and to hide among them
until their ship has sailed away. But in clawing their way down from
the heights, they stumble into the wrong valley. They find themselves
among the Typees: cannibals so fierce that they are a terror to all who
know of them. Miraculously, for reasons that Melville is never able to
divine, he and his friend Toby are given a friendly welcome by this

tribe, and they settle down to a life as honored guests. Yet they prove to be prisoners as much as guests, kept under constant surveillance by their hosts, and prevented from moving about freely.

Because Melville is suffering from a bloated, apparently infected leg, Toby is eventually allowed to seek help. He is tricked aboard a ship in need of hands, though, and never returns. Ignorant of Toby's fate, Melville cannot be sure of his own. Nevertheless, in the intermissions of his understandable fears, he manages to savor the pleasures of what turns out to be a veritably paradisal valley.

There follows the memorable heart of the book. Melville describes a life of lazily sensuous pleasures far removed from his latest contact with civilization: the rigid, regimented economy of shipboard. With a beautiful native girl, Fayaway, he loafs, bathes, eats, cavorts. In paradisal Typee, rules and restrictions come to seem supererogatory. Observing no instances of theft, Melville concludes that he has found an egalitarian society where laws are unnecessary. The only work a Typee performs in the course of his life is the planting of a single breadfruit tree for each of his offspring. This and other fruits are abundant in the lowlands that they inhabit, and the sea yields up its harvest when the men are of a mind to fish. Sensuality is unfettered. The women take several husbands without arousing any apparent signs of jealousy. A physically beautiful people, the Typees live in what looks like perfect natural health. All in all the chief ills of Western civilization seem to be absent: scarcity, poverty, competition, repression.

The dramatic and philosophical question raised by *Typee* is why, despite all this, Melville decides to escape. When a ship appears in the bay, he resolves to show himself. Many of the Typees—the fiercest among them it would seem—now want to prevent him from approaching the water. But for the first time some of them display what appears to be sympathy for his plight, and help him hobble and be carried in that direction. They will not let him approach the ship's boat, though, until his part is unexpectedly taken by Marheyo, the somewhat senile old native who has been his host. "He placed his arm upon my shoulder, and emphatically pronounced the only two English words I had taught him: 'Home' and 'Mother.'" This first act of imaginative projection by a Typee is followed by Melville's one act of brutality. He hastily clambers onto the boat. Then, when he is pursued by the horrific, one-eyed chief, Mow Mow, who had led the opposition to his release, Melville makes good his escape by plunging a boat hook just below the native's throat.

This richly paradoxical ending creates feelings of both inevitability and regret. Old Marheyo's unexpected projection of sympathy beyond his time-bound world raises the possibility of a genuine meeting of cultures, yet his insight is limited, making Melville's departure seem inevitable. Melville has deplored the Western relationship to the islanders, pointing out how sailors and missionaries brought with them diseases and instruments of war that decimated native cultures. Now his own blow for freedom puts him in just such a relationship to the Typees.

It is not surprising that certain early readers of *Typee* failed to appreciate its ambiguities. Some early reviewers rigidly lined themselves up as advocates for either civilization or primitivism, quite ignoring Melville's balanced distribution of right and wrong, advantages and disadvantages. Starting with the rediscovery of Melville's works in the 1920s, modern critics left partisanship far behind. Then, surprisingly, the terms of the old debate were revived in the 1970s. This time, though, there was no one on the scene to represent civilization.

As a result, *Typee* has come to be regarded by recent critics as an unwavering indictment of civilization, as much so in its ending as anywhere else. Does Melville describe there a scene of agonized parting from Fayaway and her family as he stands on the beach waiting for rescue? This only demonstrates a "betrayal of his loved ones." * Is Melville forced into an act of violence to save his life? This "demonstrates the universal trait of savagery." Or, still worse, his act teaches that "civilization has succeeded only in magnifying and developing a basic savagery which is found in a less appalling form in a primitive culture."

Opinions such as these, in which the critics find civilization being exposed as worse than primitive life everywhere in *Typee*, are virtually the only ones currently to be found in academic journals and in

---

* Edgar A. Dryden, *Melville's Thematics of Form: The Great Art of Telling the Truth* (Johns Hopkins University Press, 1968). The chapter on *Typee* is printed—along with early reviews, other essays, a bibliography of writings on *Typee*, and an introductory survey of *Typee* criticism by the editor—in *Critical Essays on Herman Melville's Typee*, ed. Milton R. Stern (G. K. Hall & Co., 1982). The quotations in the present essay come from this volume and other sources. Full documentation may be found in the *New Criterion* version of the essay.

books published by university presses. Such publications, it should be noted, are routinely scrutinized and approved by panels of scholars.

Such a loss of confidence in and esteem for civilization is not unprecedented. In *Civilization and Its Discontents,* Freud described a built-in resentment at the restraints that accompany civilization. Civilized man constantly chafes against these restraints, and is always tempted to repudiate them. During at least two periods in history, Freud suggests, man's accumulated resentments have issued in outright condemnations of civilization. The first of these periods followed the birth of Christianity, and the second the age of exploration. *Typee,* itself a travel book, came at the end of the second period, and capitalized on both contemporary romanticization of the noble savage and a reigniting of the universal urge to flee civilization. It would appear that a third period of the kind drawn attention to by Freud had its birth in the countercultural revolution of the 1960s. One of the fruits of this latter revolution was the repudiation of norms that become a staple of literary discourse in the 1970s and 1980s.

From the beginning those reviewers who emphasized Melville's indictments of civilization spoke in the name of social reform. Writing for the Fourierist *Harbinger* of Brook Farm, the utopian community where Nathaniel Hawthorne had briefly resided a few years earlier, John Sullivan Dwight compared the unfettered, communal existence of the Typees with the evils of civilization arising from economic exploitation. Defending civilization were Christian conservatives stimulated in part by resentment at Melville's criticisms of the missionary enterprise. William Oland Bourne of the *Christian Parlor Magazine* wrote a review that Milton R. Stern, the foremost modern critic of *Typee,* has described as "grim, humorless, and righteous." In it, Bourne admits that the bringing of civilization to the islands had its unfortunate consequences. But he accuses Melville of giving a distorted picture by alternately ignoring and temporizing over the "degraded and benighted" practices of the islanders. That such distortion might be part of Melville's literary intention did not occur to Bourne. Nevertheless, he caught Melville in contradictions that can no more be justified from a literary point of view than from a logical or moral one.

The humorlessness and lack of literary sophistication of Bourne and subsequent Christian reviewers have permitted modern critics to

108   AMERICAN LITERATURE

dismiss their arguments. Not so Melville, though, who evidently read Bourne's review with care. For example, Bourne pointed out that in his narration Melville both protested the use of the word *savages* and demonstrated its appropriateness, in one instance following his complaint with an example of native behavior that justified such usage in the very next paragraph. Melville proceeded to remove both paragraphs (along with rephrasings of several descriptions too explicit in their sexual details). These changes appeared in a second American edition a few months after the first. Their fate at the hands of modern editors, a group with no apparent allegiance to either side in the civilization-primitivism controversy, reveals how far scholarly capitulation to civilization's discontents has progressed in recent years.

At Northwestern University an edition of Melville's works based on modern principles of scholarly editing has been coming out since 1968. Its editors have seen fit to reject Melville's revisions. To do so they rest their case, as far as one can make out, on the fact that Melville revised *Typee* at the request of his publisher. Yet the rules of modern editing enjoin acceptance of an author's "final intentions," which is to say his last set of revisions, whether or not they have come at someone else's behest. No rule is without its exceptions, to be sure. But adherence to an author's final intentions is so central to the contemporary editorial enterprise that one is surprised to find an exception being made under almost any circumstances. And still more surprising is it that the breaking of the rule is hardly discussed in the two elaborate and lengthy scholarly essays that accompany the Northwestern edition—essays containing exhaustive discussion and justification for virtually every comma inserted or removed by the editors.

One of the editors candidly reports that in writing to his publisher Melville "strongly implied that his revisions were thoughtful and voluntary." In order to lend "a unity to the book which it wanted before," he had decided to remove those passages that were "altogether foreign to the adventure." In these and similar remarks not cited by the editors, Melville made it clear that he was satisfied with his changes. Subsequently, furthermore, though he had no need to mollify English public opinion, which was put off neither by *Typee*'s sexual explicitness nor its criticisms of American missionaries, Melville attempted to persuade his English publisher to make the same cuts. "The permanent reputation as well as the present popularity of Typee," he argued, "will be greatly promoted by the revision." Yet not even this appeal to the primacy of aesthetic form—something usually dear to the twentieth-century sensibility—could deter the Northwestern editors from rejecting the revisions.

It is a maxim in the study of intellectual history that the faith of each historical period lies hidden in its unargued assumptions. Such is the case at hand. The Northwestern editors assumed that contemporary objections to Melville's remarks about religion or his treatment of sex could only reflect the religious intolerance and sexual prudery of the nineteenth century. Under the circumstances their breach of rules to restore passages critical of civilization and religion, along with sexually explicit passages, presented itself as self-evidently enlightened.

In the 1950s Richard Chase, Milton Stern, and a few other critics developed an approach to *Typee* that had the incidental result of honoring Melville's final intentions. For by concentrating on what Melville had termed "the intrinsick merit of the narrative alone," they effectively made the discursive passages less important. Chase, the author of the seminal *The American Novel and Its Tradition* as well as a book on Melville, was one of the outstanding scholar-critics of his age. Stern is a leading scholarly authority on Melville, and is most recently the editor of a collection of essays on *Typee*. Along with other critics of the 1950s, Chase and Stern began to treat *Typee* as a work of fiction. Scholarship had demonstrated that Melville's account was substantially accurate, its fictionalization amounting for the most part to a heightening of romantic details and a claim to have spent several more weeks in Typee than was probably the case. On the other hand it was possible to argue that Melville the narrator was not quite identical with the Melville who experienced the adventure. The latter, furthermore, introduces himself to the Typees as "Tom," a single syllable that he thinks they will have less trouble pronouncing than his own name. They can only say it as "Tommo," however, and from the point of view of some literary critics the resultant false name given to Melville amounts to his being fictionalized into a character.

Once *Typee* became a fictional work, it was but a small step to

seeing it as a symbolic one as well. The primitivism-civilization conundrum could now be resolved, not by Melville's philosophizings,
but chiefly with reference to the needs of Tommo's personal development and through the interpretable meanings of such symbols as his
infected leg. So long as *Typee* had been regarded as a straightforward
memoir, Melville's leg appeared as simply one more detail of his adventure. Now Richard Chase noted that the leg improved while
Tommo enjoyed the pleasures of Typee but swelled up again when
the natives threatened to cover him with tattoos. The pain, as Stern
agreed, was a call back to civilization.

By treating *Typee* as a fictional and symbolic work, Stern and
Chase were able to remove any unpleasant, chauvinistic overtones
from Tommo's choice in favor of civilization. Their approach, however, opened the door to a rejection of this choice by their successors.
Thus a typical critic of the 1970s no longer accepted the return to
civilization as defensible. *Typee* became nothing more than "a com-
prehensive satire which unmasks the damned and damning intellect
of the Western mind itself." As for Melville's leg, "if the swelling is a
symbol at all," another critic writes, "it probably signifies his *attraction* to Typee" (italics in original). For still another critic the pain
serves not as a reminder of home but rather "points in fact to Tommo's inability to embrace physicality, an inability which flows from
his having been infected by Western consciousness, reason, and intel-
lectuality." And this critic adds: "The fact that Tommo's attraction
towards these things is symbolized by a painful infection should be
sufficient evidence of Melville's judgment of their ultimate worth."

As these last remarks suggest, once Tommo had been disassoci-
ated from Melville, any loyalty to civilization found in the narrative
could be dismissed as an expression of his failings as a character. Accordingly, Tommo was now described as suffering from "sexual perversion and self-conceit," and as "selfish and so egocentric that he
must impose his will wherever he is." Finally, Tommo is indicted by
selective omission in the following account of his escape: "One Typeean does not want to let Tommo leave the island. He swims after
Tommo, and Tommo smashes a boat hook into the savage's throat.
This, the tale's single scene of violence, concludes Tommo's story."
Tommo is the violent one, the swimming native presumably a kind
of disappointed host. But in fact the character who "does not want

to let Tommo leave" has indicated his reluctance by hurling a javelin at those on board the rowboat Melville has entered. "Swims after Tommo" omits to mention that this native grips a tomahawk in his teeth, leads a group of swimmers shouting their intention to devour the pursued, and is about to grapple the oars—"the maneuver which has proved so fatal to many a boat's crew in these seas."

In retrospect it is apparent that, though by the 1950s one no longer proclaimed the superiority of civilization, one continued to assume it. Thus, consciously or not, when Stern criticized the "primitive savagery of the western ship's crews," he was implicitly measuring their behavior against Western civilized norms, and not those of the South Pacific. Similarly, Stern was free to accept Melville's indictment of the West because he never imagined its being employed to repudiate Western values.

At present the consensus that underlay the original fictional and symbolic readings of *Typee* no longer exists. It has been replaced among literary critics by an unremitting cultural self-loathing. The words *savagery* and *civilization* have come to be used only with quotation marks—"civilization" to separate oneself from a supposedly self-centered, delusory conviction of cultural superiority, and "savagery" to imply that the term is nothing more than an expression of Western ethnocentrism. As one critic explains, Melville "saw that savagery was a term applicable to the Europeans' colonial and missionary activities in the Pacific rather than to the people they practiced upon." At present the only acceptable use of the terms in question is in phrases such as "the savagery of civilization," which is used by another critic of the same persuasion.

It is true that in *Typee* Melville exclaims, "How often is the term 'savages' incorrectly applied!" And Melville also argues that Westerners have "exasperated" the South Sea islanders "into savages." The remark and the argument, however, both appear in the first of the two contradictory paragraphs pointed out by William Oland Bourne. In the remainder of *Typee*, when Melville employed the term *savages*—some two dozen times—he did so in just the manner his own early paragraph complained of. Thus his narration refers to "savage resentment," "the fickle disposition of savages," an ever-present fear of "the savage nature of the beings at whose mercy I was," and "the craft [i.e., craftiness] peculiar to savages." Elsewhere Melville's adjectives are "simple," "unsophisticated," "heathenish," and "treacherous" savages. Given the choice between bringing these references in line with his complaint about misusage and bringing the complaint in line with them, Melville, as we know, chose to remove the paragraphs singled out by Bourne. In addition, he went so far as to strike out the few phrases in his book that were in *accord* with that paragraph: the similarly apologetic "those whom we call savages" and "noble savage" used as an honorific.

As with *savages,* so with *cannibalism,* a seemingly unambiguous term that has acquired both quotation marks and a party of apologists. This time the exaggerated mode of early reviewers was never entirely set aside. Thus with a laudable intent to oppose Western cultural self-congratulation, an anonymous early English reviewer fell into blatant illogic:

> The Polynesians have the advantage of the cannibals of civilised life, for we have long since made the pleasant discovery, that man-eating is not confined to the Anthropophagi of the South Seas. The latter have undoubtedly one redeeming distinction— they can only devour their enemies slain in battle: there is nothing which man in a civilised state has a keener appetite for than his particular friend.

Stern unfortunately perpetuated this kind of verbal imprecision by referring to the scrounging for edibles aboard Melville's ship when stores were low as an example of "western spoilation and cannibalism." This is a highly emotional way to describe eating the captain's pig.

Stern's successors, again taking matters further than he could have anticipated, used the same kind of imprecision to emphasize not the inhumanity of individual Westerners but rather the culpability of their nations as a whole. Playing on the same word *devour,* one critic now asked, "who are the real cannibals, the Typees who practice a ritual of eating the flesh of their dead attackers or the aggressor nations who have come to devour the islands?" But this is not all: cannibalism has also found its positive defenders.

For some critics the self-evident superiority of primitive life is in itself a sufficient justification of the practice. "The Typees occasionally indulge in headhunting and cannibalism," one of them genially concedes. But more important is their possession of the "one valuable commodity of human existence—happiness." More sophisticated critics begin by reducing cannibalism to the status of a literary trope: "the narrative's central metaphor for the primitive's threat to consume Tommo's contemporary identity." One of these, who has already indicated that he is dubious about the very existence of cannibalism among the Typees, concludes, "Whether or not the Typees are literal cannibals, they are certainly figurative cannibals that are devouring Melville's historical identity."

When it comes to cannibalism the fictional Tommo, who has already been impugned on other grounds, is judged to be so hysterical on the subject that his testimony can be safely laid aside. "There is no evidence the Typeeans actually plan to eat Tommo," one critic states with equanimity. Writes another, "He can never rid himself of his fear of their reported cannibalistic practices, although, in fact, he experiences only comfort at their hands." Five recent critics agree that the true problem lies in Tommo's own character. Critic number one has it that in his estimate of the Typees "the impulse to fix on the practice of cannibalism as typifying their character is presented as a feature of Tommo's state of mind." Critic number two writes: "His exaggerated fears of cannibalism, his horror of tattooing . . . and his repeated attempts to escape his kindly captors suggest that something must be wrong with Tommo." Critic number three refers to "his fear of cannibalism, which he insists upon keeping alive in himself although he is never threatened by it." Number four: "Cannibalism perfectly embodies Tommo's primitive fears, for the island has awakened the boundaryless, devouring infant within him." And number five, who refers to the illusions not of Tommo but of Melville himself: "Melville may not actually have feared cannibalism, but he seems to have been plagued by psychosomatic symptoms of tension."

The only possibility not entertained by these critics is that a man isolated among known cannibals might fear for his life. What calls for explanation is the psychology of Melville's reluctance to face the realities of Typee, as evidenced in his managing to ignore cannibalism during the intermissions of his fears. Eventually, as the Typees grow importunate to impose on him what Melville terms "the hideous blemish of tattooing," he recognizes their determination to adopt him as one of them. Now he is in danger not so much of being eaten as of having to join in the eating of human flesh—a quite sufficient reason to seek escape that has also not occurred to the critics.

As it happens, just two years after the appearance of *Typee,* an account of another recent sojourn among the Marquesans was published by one William Torrey, like Melville a young sailor who jumped ship. Torrey, too, was held as an unwilling guest—for eighteen months. During this time he found it necessary to preserve his life by submitting to being tattooed (on the hands), and then to eating human flesh.

But for some critics it is not enough to deny that Tommo is in danger. He is indicted as well for failing to appreciate the *virtues* of cannibalism. That practice, it is explained, is actually a "ritual"—than which there is no higher term of approbation in contemporary literary criticism. Cannibalism intends only the ritual "ingestion of the enemy's virtue," one critic explains. Thus, we suffer from "a false understanding of cannibalism" if, like Tommo, we regard it simply as a matter of killing and eating. For when Tommo sees "first shrunken heads, and then a skeleton in a box to which cling morsels passed over by sated feeders," these "focusing images" serve to expose his inadequate view of cannibalism—an act that "is less a dietary practice than a ritual ingestion of the antagonist's virtue." The benighted Tommo, the argument continues, fails to recognize that the cannibal "is therefore mindful of the individuality of the vanquished." Indeed, the virtues of cannibalism are precisely those calculated to expose Tommo's failures of humanism:

> The true difference between Tommo's and the Typees' views of cannibalism is that he considers individuality to be completely free of its vessel, and so concludes that to eat the body is to express contempt for the self: whereas they treat the body as a rich and necessary participant in the personality that is indissociably immured in its texture.

"So much for decadent Western dualism," one imagines Cannibal A remarking to Cannibal B as the two perform their richly integrative act.

The critics' apologies for cannibalism clash not only with common sense but also with Melville's treatment of the subject throughout *Typee*. For, far from celebrating cannibalism as ritual, Melville refers to the practice much as he does to "savages." His expressions are "many a horrid rite," "the frightful genius of native worship," and "irreclaimable cannibals." Read selectively, it is true, *Typee* can be made to yield up a defense of cannibalism as well as of savagery. Early in the book, for example, Melville dismisses the charge that the Typees trapped and ate white sailors, claiming that they ate only the flesh of their enemies (not their "slain attackers," with its implication that all Typeean battles were defensive). In the scene of discovering the human remains, though, Melville realizes that inasmuch as the severed heads before him have been hanging overhead in pots since his arrival, they cannot belong to recently killed enemy warriors as his hosts insist. "It was plain," Melville writes, "that I had seen the last relic of some unfortunate wretch, who must have been massacred on the beach by the savages, in one of those perilous trading adventures which I have before described." It is at this point that Melville—or if one prefers, Tommo—expresses the fear for his life that contemporary critics are united in dismissing.

To be sure, the critics base their apologies for cannibalism not only on Melville, but also on the evidence of modern anthropology. Yet this evidence, too, proves to be very different from what they imagine. As Melville's discovery scene indicates, cannibalism was *not* limited to the ingestion of the enemy's virtue. One learns from anthropology, furthermore, that the Typeeans ate children as well as adults, their own tribesmen as well as enemies (and hapless strangers found on the beach). Furthermore, human flesh was eaten not only in ritual, but also as part of the Typeean diet. Nor was the act of cannibalizing limited to warriors, as in some other South Sea islands. It was practiced by women and children as well as men. As for the enemies among those who were eaten, these were by no means limited to battle casualties being used in celebrations of victory: "[Cannibalistic] sacrifices occurred when victims were available at all life-crisis rites of high-status individuals, particularly death, for warfare, to break droughts, to improve harvests, and to ensure the success of constructions." The permanent state of war (of which Melville was aware) applied equally to the Typees and their neighbors. It involved every man, woman, and child's fear of being taken captive, tortured, and eaten whenever ritual victims were required, a situation that prevailed virtually all of the time.

As to what took place at these rituals, the fragmentary details available throw a ghastly light on the apologetics of contemporary literary critics. Tortures prior to immolation could last for several days. "In cases where a victim was taken alive," a modern anthropologist reveals, "parts of his body would often be carved, cooked, and eaten before his eyes." At other times, "eyes were often eaten raw." Dreadful tortures, the eating of children, a life punctuated by cannibal feasts: these are the realities of Typeean life. They make it possible to answer with some confidence the question "Who are the real cannibals?"

Literary critics have had fun with the inflated rhetoric of "degraded and benighted practices" used by nineteenth-century moralists like William Oland Bourne. Melville himself disarmed his reader by joking at the beginning of *Typee* about "cannibal banquets" and, in humorous italics, "*heathenish rites and human sacrifices.*" By the end of the book, though, these phrases take on a deadly seriousness. In view of the narrator's discovery of human remains (and the anthropological reality behind it), the genuine shock of nineteenth-century man, albeit pompously expressed, does him more credit than the contemporary literary critic's unflappable sophistication.

To be sure, the attempt to gloss over cannibalism goes all the way back to Montaigne. Up through the nineteenth century, though, it was possible to regard cannibalism as an anomalous, infrequently encountered, minor blot on otherwise ideal societies. Today, we know—or ought to know—that cannibalism is no anomaly, and is by no means the only defect of the societies in which it appears. Freud observed in *Civilization and Its Discontents* that primitive peoples are subject to "restrictions of a different kind but perhaps of greater severity than those attaching to modern civilized man." He had in mind the operations of taboo, well described by Melville and identified clearly enough in *Typee* as a system too restrictive for a free-thinking Westerner to survive in. "The savage," Melville writes of the taboo, "lives in the continual observance of its dictates, which guide and control every action of his being."

Both the taboo and other restrictions among the Typees extended to their fabled sexual freedom and openness. In each family the appearance of unfettered lovemaking hinted at by Melville was, it develops, belied by the chief husband's control over sexual access to his wife by secondary husbands. The system of multiple husbands and lovers for the women, by the way, hardly supports the contention that Melville's flight from Typee was an "abandonment of loved ones." He could hardly have maintained his romantic relationship with Fayaway on Typee except as a pauper and virtual outcast in society. This is because wealth and status came from attracting subordinate husbands to share one's wife.

The psychoanalyst Abram Kardiner suggested that as a result of the chief husband's control, most Typeean males nurtured a suppressed jealousy. This found its expression in a resentment of women reflected in certain taboos and in the culture's folklore. For example, women were forbidden by taboo to enter canoes. Their genitals could render taboo any objects which they passed over. The apparently enviable sexual activity available to women was, like much else in the culture, not entirely a matter of free choice. Ritual sexual dancing followed by public sexual intercourse was regarded as a woman's "religious obligation." Similarly, Typeean children were sexually uninhibited, but a girl's introduction to sex was often by rape: an eighteenth-century traveler witnessed a girl of eight being held down by four women and made to undergo intercourse.

Melville experienced some of the coercive tendencies of Typee society, but he did not recognize the degree to which these were modulated during his stay. For he had stumbled upon a scarcity economy at a time of remission from its problem of food supply. Though there were no visible signs at the time, the Typees were actually subject to periodic famines. Soon after the islands had come under European observation some years before Melville's arrival, a famine had lasted from 1803 to 1813, wiping out an estimated two-thirds of the population. Except for the privileged few, the best the society had been able to devise in preparation for its six- and seven-year droughts was a method of storing a one or two years' breadfruit supply. There was neither any Typee agriculture (as Melville did note), nor any provision for feeding the tribe's pigs, nor means devised to harvest enough protein from the abundant ocean.

The great feasts, contributing to the impression of abundance reported by Melville and others, were actually expressions of anxiety reflecting far leaner years in the past. Similarly, the resentful taboos on females reflected an accompanying belief in their responsibility for scarcity. As other early travelers reported, in order to bring rain when the breadfruit failed, a young girl was brought forth and publicly strangled to death by her brother. And during a famine in 1797, "the natives amused themselves" by administering a slight push to a starving, staggering woman and then watching as she toppled to the ground.

It is sometimes argued that the acts of the Typees and other natives occur on a small scale, whereas the depredations of Westerners, particularly venereal disease, have amounted, as one critic put it, to "genocide." Yet the unfortunate ravages caused by the transmission of venereal disease from the West, aside from falling short of genocide, were entirely inadvertent. In contrast, the Typees conducted "full fledged wars of extermination." In an amphibious assault on a nearby island they put to death the entire population of a rival tribe—an act of conscious, successful genocide.

One could go on. The list of misconceptions about the Typees covers most of what the critics think they know about them. Sacrificial torture, killing, and cannibalizing were normally carried out only on behalf of the "well placed," a circumstance that refutes the idea of an egalitarian society. Though material objects were not subject to theft, as Melville indicated, unbeknownst to him the theft of food was common. The Typees were most certainly a beautiful, physically robust people. But the analysis of burial remains shows a high incidence of arthritis as early in life as adolesence.

Given the increase in anthropological knowledge about the shortcomings of Typeean culture, the concurrent increase in self-delusion among literary critics calls for some explanation. In the 1970s the liberal and radical politics that had from the beginnings of *Typee* criticism been associated with cultural relativism and celebration of the primitive were adapted to the terms of contemporary politics. Melville's book came to be associated with charges of imperialist war upon and subjugation of Third World peoples. The critic who used the term *aggressor nations* meant by it "capitalist nations." The critic who found alienation in Tommo's psychology related it to "the alienation of labor in industrial society."

More up-to-date, another critic has refined the meaning of "exploitation" as it applies to the West in general and Tommo in particular. Without accusing Tommo of taking economic advantage of the Typees, this critic charges him with *mentally* using them for his own selfish purposes. Tommo's contrasting of his own culture with theirs is condemned as an act of "imaginative imperialism." By using the Typees in an argument, it is explained, Tommo makes himself "complicit in the [Western] brutality he claims to deplore." Thus the civilized man's habit of thought is treated as a brutal crime, whereas the primitive's actual brutalities are termed features of an "independent cultural coherence." All this, moreover, is assumed to have been "deliberately" implied by Melville.

On the contrary, Melville was at once less ideological and more subversive than his recent critics imagine. Their tendency is to justify the discontents of civilization. In contrast, *Typee* plunges the reader directly into the disturbing experience of those discontents. The reader subsequently accepts Melville's abrupt return to civilization, but only reluctantly. The lingering impression left by *Typee* is one of unfettered pleasures. Irate defenses of civilization in the manner of William Oland Bourne, and denunciations of it as capitalistic in the manner of the latest critics, equally violate the literary integrity of Melville's work.

Criticism properly enters the picture on a different level. Its first responsibility is to honor the literary experience, its second to relocate the frequently subversive thrust of that experience in the context of more permanent values. In times of cultural upheaval such as the 1960s these tasks come to seem particularly onerous. Criticism grows unpopular with critics themselves. Some of them claim literature's privilege of immersion in the destructive element. Still others subordinate their critical understanding to their political convictions. They prove to abandon their literary responsibilities in favor of political denunciation. On another level, editors prepare texts under the broad influence of the same attitudes.

Underlying these attitudes is a cultural relativism that, while supposedly grounded in anthropologically sophisticated insight, actually rests on an anthropological double standard. Toward the primitive, a stance of nonjudgmental scientific objectivity is assumed; toward the civilized, one of subjective morality. The confident ethnocentrism of native cultures is admired, but the very right to exist of one's own culture is denied. So powerful have the imperatives of relativism grown, in fact, that not only can the norms of logic be suspended in its service, but also the cultivated sensibility that turns us away in disgust from cannibalism. For the critics of *Typee,* virtually any abandonment of values has been preferable to admitting an allegiance to civilization.

The New Criterion, January 1985

THE DECLINE
OF STANDARDS

PLAGIARISM
AND THE
LITERARY
CONSCIENCE

=======

IN THE PAST FEW YEARS a number of prominent writers have been accused of plagiarism, among them Norman Mailer (for his first book on Marilyn Monroe), Alex Haley (for *Roots*), John Gardner (for a biography of Chaucer), Dee Brown (for *Bury My Heart at Wounded Knee*), Penelope Gilliatt (for her *New Yorker* profile of Graham Greene), Ken Follett (for his spy novel, *The Key to Rebecca*), and Gail Sheehy (for *Passages*). More recently, Martin Amis, the son of Kingsley Amis, charged that his 1973 novel, *The Rachel Papers*, had been plagiarized by Jacob Epstein, a twenty-three-year-old first novelist.

As far as one can tell, none of these writers suffered from the resultant publicity. Instead, a universal reluctance to render judgment meant that even those of them who confessed were never publicly disgraced. As Edgar Allan Poe was the first to observe, "When a plagiarism is detected, it generally happens that the public sympathy is with the plagiarist." It can be added that most of the embarrassment in such cases is ordinarily experienced not so much by the accused as by those who have been confronted by his deed. Thus reporters and editorialists tend to replace the word *plagiarism* with uneasy euphemisms. *Newsweek,* for example, put it that Alex Haley "acknowledged *lifting* modest portions of *Roots*"; that the film critic Penelope Gilliatt was caught "appropriating another author's eloquence"; and that

John Gardner "was discovered to have *borrowed lavishly*" (all italics added).

After an initial flurry of discussion, most charges of plagiarism tend to disappear from public view. If a suit and trial follow, the result is usually a private, unrecorded settlement, part of which is an agreement not to publicize the outcome. The writings in question remain extant, of course, but no one is eager to evaluate them.

The contrast could not be sharper between the literary world's failure to render judgment and the Draconian code imposed by the scientific community. When Dr. Vijay Soman was recently discovered to have plagiarized some sixty words in a medical paper, for example, he was forced to resign his position at Yale University. Soman, it is true, was at first given only a mild rebuke. But the persistence of the researcher who had accused him led to an investigation in which it developed that he had faked data in addition to plagiarizing, and as a result he was asked to leave.

Later, Soman's superior, Dr. Philip Felig, had to resign his recent appointment as chairman of the department of medicine at Columbia's College of Physicians and Surgeons. Although Dr. Felig was not himself accused of either plagiarism or faking data, the people who had interviewed him for the Columbia chairmanship felt in retrospect that he had kept his faith in Soman for too long a time and had given a too generous account of Soman's improprieties. Dr. Felig was eventually rehired, but by Yale, not Columbia.

To be sure, one senses in Dr. Felig's delayed response the same reluctance to come to terms with the problem as that displayed by humanists. In numerous cases of scientific plagiarism and fraud over the past few years, as Alan F. Westin of Columbia University has shown, the perpetrators have suffered less than those who exposed them. When a plagiarism is detected, it seems, the public's sympathy for the plagiarist is often matched by its disapproval of the victim. Nevertheless, even the most reluctant authorities cannot avoid taking action when science is in question, whereas in literary studies it is possible to avoid the unpleasant responsibility of dealing with a breach of ethics.

This avoidance would seem to be related to the attacks on literary standards that have come from various sources in recent years. One school of literary critics, for example, has argued that all professional literary interpretations are merely subjective, so that no critic or criticism is really any better than any other. Another school has seized on a contention put forward by the critic Harold Bloom, who maintains that poets are so much influenced by their predecessors, unconsciously as well as consciously, that no poet can be called original. Commenting on Bloom's list of six ways in which influence supposedly exerts itself in poetry, one sympathetic scholar, Thomas McFarland, has logically suggested that "he might have added a seventh, 'plagiarism.'"

McFarland elsewhere voices the "hope" that modern relativism has so far freed us from the "rigid certainties of Victorian moralism" as to make it no longer necessary to be terribly concerned about plagiarism. In contrast, it was not very long ago that a historian of the subject could still regard plagiarism as both a moral and a cultural issue. In *Literary Ethics* (1928), H. M. Paull posited the importance of knowing the extent to which plagiarism is being practiced at a given time. Furthermore, "the extent to which it is condoned," he argued, "is a still more valuable indication of the state of the literary conscience of the period."

Currently, the tendency in the literary world is either to deny or to extenuate the commission of plagiarism. Where the act in a given instance proves to be too overt to be denied, it is typically described as an exception—a plagiarism by technicality only. In effect, plagiarism has come to be regarded as a relative phenomenon—one to which disgrace no longer attaches. Writers have always plagiarized, it is said. Shakespeare and other greats, we are reminded, explicitly justified themselves with the concept of "imitation," by which writers were positively encouraged to model their works on those of their predecessors. In accusing Jacob Epstein of plagiarism, Martin Amis himself, for reasons that will appear, softened his indictment by remarking that "the boundary between influence and plagiarism will always be vague." All in all it begins to seem that plagiarism amounts to no more than the invidious relabeling of practices that were once perfectly acceptable.

How much, in fact, has the definition of plagiarism changed through history? At present, plagiarism is defined as the wrongful taking of and representing as one's own the ideas, words, or inventions of another. In the ancient world and through the neoclassical period of the seventeenth and eighteenth centuries, imitation was admittedly the prescribed mode of composition. Writers were expected to adopt models for their work and to follow these with regard to plot, characters, and even versification and expression. It was only with the Romantics of the late eighteenth and early nineteenth centuries that originality came to be valued over imitation. Not surprisingly, concern about plagiarism greatly increased during the Romantic period and continued, along with the high valuation of originality, down to the quite recent past.

Yet it does not follow, as some have argued, that plagiarism is a strictly modern concept. The poet Martial complained of being plagiarized from in the first century A.D. The term *plagiary* itself entered the English language in the sixteenth century, along with bitter accusations by writers against one another. The concept of plagiarism, therefore, existed alongside that of imitation, so that there have always been acceptable and unacceptable modes of using the work of one's predecessors. What has not changed through time is the ethic of borrowing. Throughout history the act of using the work of another *with an intent to deceive* has been branded as plagiarism. As Lord Chesterfield pithily phrased it in the eighteenth century, a plagiarist is "a man that steals other people's thoughts and puts 'em off for his own."

There will always remain certain gray areas resistant to definition. Not every act of copying from another author is the same, for example, since a wider latitude is traditionally allowed for imitating authors of the past. This was the case with Shakespeare's use of Plutarch, and also with John Updike in an example cited by *Newsweek* as evidence that plagiarism is virtually universal among writers. "Even John Updike," *Newsweek* noted, "recalls comfortingly that 'my first published novel was very clearly an imitation of Henry James.'" Yet one can imagine Updike's following his well-known, virtually classical model as closely, say, as Joyce followed the *Odyssey* in *Ulysses* without raising any question of plagiarism. On the other hand, equally extensive, unacknowledged use of a contemporary's work—with the intent to deceive—would have to be labeled plagiarism.

When one turns to recently publicized accusations of plagiarism, the authors' explanations at first seem to support the notion that plagiarism cannot be satisfactorily defined. For example, Alex Haley was sued by two novelists, Margaret Walker Alexander and Harold Courlander, the latter the author of *The African*. Haley swore that he had not read *The African* but admitted that three passages from it had "found their way" into *Roots*. Jacob Epstein was more forthright about the accusation that he had taken more than fifty passages from Martin Amis's novel. But though Epstein freely admitted having "taken another writer's imagery and language for my novel" (*Wild Oats*, 1979), he blamed his doing so on faulty record keeping. Similarly, when Dee Brown was accused of improperly taking materials (for *Bury My Heart at Wounded Knee* in fourteen separate instances) from the historian Lawrence Kelly, he admitted only that "six sentences were taken from Kelly, and omission of the source was an oversight of the typist."

Both Haley and Epstein said that they had collected passages in notebooks without keeping track of where they came from. Then, long after copying them out, they had inadvertently used them in their books. Haley said that he used notebooks containing passages originally copied by his research assistants as well as by himself. Epstein added that he himself had discovered his borrowings after publication, and had in fact removed thirteen of them from the second American edition of his novel.

All of these cases at first appear to offer insuperable problems of definition—until it is noticed that each of the explanations contains an admission of wrongdoing. Those accused do not actually deny that plagiarism took place; instead, they suggest that extenuating circumstances should make us hesitate to render judgment. At issue, they argue, are nothing but a few inadvertent, unconscious slips. Thus if there was plagiarism, it was neither extensive nor intended.

Can plagiarism take place inadvertently, unconsciously? Certainly every writer worries that he may unconsciously be echoing, or even repeating, phrases or ideas that have somehow stuck in his mind. Similarly, researchers fear that inadvertent mistakes in footnoting may have resulted in their failure to credit all of their sources properly. The feeling that one may unconsciously be a sinner oneself makes writers especially hesitant to pronounce judgment on other writers who have been accused of plagiarism. But while it is theoretically possible for anyone to breach the rules inadvertently, for the most part the incompletely or improperly attributed passages in the working author's manuscript somehow are caught by the time his work sees print. It may happen that an observer will later point out an uncredited idea or phrase, but there will be no implication of plagiarism.

This is because an accusation of plagiarism normally arises only where there has been a *pattern* of improper conduct. Practically speaking, authors are sued, not for single acts of plagiarism, though technically they could be, but for having committed *dozens* of such acts. Any one failure to acknowledge a source might be defended, were it not that the pattern of which it is a part points to an intent to deceive. Accordingly, the accused plagiarist, along with offering excuses, ordinarily proceeds to reduce the number of instances of wrongdoing that he has been accused of. Thus Haley reduced Courlander's "more than eighty passages" to three; Dee Brown reduced fourteen to six; Epstein reduced more than forty to thirteen. The writers plagiarized from—reasoning that, having extracted a confession of plagiarism, they have no need to quibble—often silently agree to the reduced number. At this point, the two or three or six instances can again begin to present a problem of definition—unless the larger pattern from which they have been cut is remembered.

When that pattern is kept in mind, one notices, for example, that it does not matter exactly when Jacob Epstein copied passages from Martin Amis's novel into his notebook. In the case of Amis's passage containing a reference to the English advice-columnist, Marje Proops, Amis had written, "I always tried to look tranquil, approachable, full of dear-Marje wisdom." Epstein changed this to read, "Billy . . . tried to appear sensible and approachable, full of Ann Landers wisdom, but with no result." (The passages are taken from Amis's article in the London *Observer*.) If Epstein made the substitution while copying from his notebook to the manuscript of his novel, the English columnist's name would have had to identify the passage to him as not being his own. If he substituted the American columnist's name as he copied from Amis to his notebook, it can only have been with the intent to plagiarize.

Not only are multiple plagiarisms within a single book common, but it frequently turns out that the plagiarist will eventually violate some other literary or extraliterary rule. The disputed meaning of Dr. Vijay Soman's six plagiarized sentences, for example, was suddenly clarified when his faked data were exposed. In the same way, the charge of plagiarism against Alex Haley took on a different coloration when it was followed by a serious charge that Haley had faked *his* data.

In a recent discussion of scientific fraud in the *New York Times*, Dr.

Elliott Osserman of Columbia University's College of Physicians and Surgeons remarked: "One goes on a presumption of honesty for the first time. If a given investigator has been suspect in his previous work, then I think it's a whole new ball game. Once suspect, always suspect."

It was difficult not to take this attitude in a recent case in which John Gardner was charged with plagiarism in what appears to have been an unfair manner. Some years ago a scholarly reviewer of Gardner's *Life and Times of Chaucer* had pointed out in *Speculum,* the journal of medieval studies, that Gardner "frequently"—and properly—cited the well-known authority *England in the Fourteenth Century,* by May McKisack. In numerous instances, however, Gardner copied long passages nearly verbatim from the same book without any acknowledgment. There could be no doubt that Gardner understood and accepted the conventions of attribution. Yet in the passages in question he copied McKisack in "close paraphrase"—that is, with slight variations of phraseology—without providing either footnotes or any other hint of what he was doing.

Here what at first might appear as a case too full of anomalies to be comprehensible actually fits two typical patterns. First there is the repeated use of and even oblique identification of a single, prominent book (though Gardner used other books in the same alternatingly proper and improper manner, according to the *Speculum* review). In such cases an odd but unmistakable tendency toward self-incrimination makes itself apparent. Secondly it develops that another charge of wrongdoing arises some years later. In such cases an objective observer cannot help but cast a jaundiced eye back on the *first* charge.

Initially, most observers find it difficult to believe that clues strewn about in an obvious manner can be anything but misguided attempts to give proper credit. Indeed, the cover-up is usually so flimsy that the term *plagiarism* hardly seems appropriate. Surely, it appears, the particular charge of improper copying that happens to have come one's way must represent some kind of exception. The truth, though, is that plagiarism remains what it is no matter how inexplicable the manner in which it may have been carried out.

As it develops, giving the game away proves to be the rule rather than the exception among plagiarists. Both in the commission of the original act and in the fantastic excuses that follow it, plagiarism is often calculated above all to result in detection. Though the means vary, one or another kind of hint, slip, or other suspicious gesture usually manages to call attention to the improper act. And here the common excuse that the act was unconscious offers a clue to the operative psychology. What was unconscious, it seems evident, was not the plagiaristic act itself, the deceptions surrounding which testify to a plentiful awareness of what was being done, but rather the desire to be caught. Martin Amis called the hints that give away the plagiarist a kind of honesty. He speculated that Jacob Epstein "in some half-conscious way, was too honest not to give a clue to his own imposture. Plagiarism is one of his book's principal themes."

Odd as it may seem, Amis's attack on Epstein itself fits into the category of inadvertent, yet somehow purposeful, self-exposure. For the fact is that Amis's own novel, *The Rachel Papers,* from which Jacob Epstein is alleged to have plagiarized, also contains the theme of plagiarism. One of the features borrowed from Amis by Epstein has to do precisely with this theme. Epstein followed Amis in making his hero what could be described as a verbal plagiarist: in both books the central character has the habit of collecting impressive things to say to girls. Amis's hero, who memorizes and repeats the words of others, is eventually caught committing a genuine plagiarism. On an English literature admissions paper he pretends that two phrases he has memorized from well-known critics are his own, and he cleverly applies these to the authors he has been assigned to write on.

Amis, too, it appears, is telling something both about plagiarism and about himself through the use of this theme in his novel. For in the course of exposing Epstein, he obliquely admitted to two plagiaristic acts of his own. In the first instance, Amis revealed that one of the phrases copied from him by Jacob Epstein actually came from Dickens. Closely following Amis, Epstein had described a man's hair as appearing like "two gray-colored, wiry wings on either side of his otherwise hairless head." Amis explained: "I am something of an idiom-magpie myself—to a reprehensible extent, perhaps. That bit about 'wiry wings,' for instance, was stolen by me from Dickens: Podsnap in *Our Mutual Friend* has 'two little light-coloured wiry wings, one on either side of his else bald head.'"

So disarming was Amis's manner that no one seems to have noticed that his revelation about the source of the "wiry wings," together with the following passage, amounted to a public confession: "I once lifted a whole paragraph of mesmeric jargon from J. G. Ballard's *The Drowned World*, and was reproved by the publisher via an alert Ballard fan. In fact, I had belatedly got verbal permission from Mr. Ballard, who is a friend and colleague. But the lapse was evidence of laziness, and a kind of moral torpor." Amis fails to specify exactly what kind of moral torpor was involved, but it can be observed that he claimed only a "belated" securing of permission. All in all it would be hard to improve on Amis's own conclusion that "the psychology of plagiarism is fascinatingly perverse: it risks, or invites, a deep shame, and there must be something of the death wish in it."

And yet it is not quite enough to speak of a death wish or some other psychological mechanism at the heart of plagiarism—any more than it is enough to demonstrate that the act can be satisfactorily defined and evaluated. For even as one calls for humanists to emulate the objectivity of scientists in dealing with plagiarism, one cannot help sympathizing with their reluctance to deal with the problem of plagiarism.

Such reluctance itself, in fact, can be shown to represent a part of the psychology of plagiarism. That psychology begins with the plagiarist's act of stealing material of the sort that his talent and intelligence would appear to make unnecessary for him. There follows his strewing of clues to bring about detection. After detection, the plagiarist offers excuses that testify to the unconscious motivation of his original act, though ordinarily without acknowledging either its breach of ethics or its obvious self-destructiveness. Finally there comes the sympathetic reaction of the public mentioned by Poe, followed by uneasiness, ambiguity, and eventual abdication of responsibility on the part of those called upon to render judgment.

Not all of this is unique to plagiarism. Similarly self-destructive behavior characterizes the social crime that plagiarism most closely resembles. This is kleptomania. The plagiarist resembles the kleptomaniac both in his evident wish to be detected and in the circumstance that what is stolen may not be needed. (With kleptomania, lack of need, we are told, is absolutely central.) Because kleptomania so evidently issues from an uncontrollable compulsion, furthermore, it tends, like plagiarism, to inspire understanding and sympathy. The comparison, though, stops here. For kleptomania does not result in any confusion over whether or not goods were stolen.

There is something at once fascinating and repellent about both of these acts. The normal response to them tends to be an instinctive recoil accompanied by a shudder of uneasiness or an uncomfortable feeling in the pit of the stomach. These are reactions that resemble nothing so much as the experience of the uncanny. In novels and short stories the uncanny is often conveyed through a character who is first mesmerized by some horrible apparition or evil deed and then overcome by an urge to flee. (Henry James's "The Jolly Corner" is such a story.) Freud pointed out that a reaction comparable to the one represented in such fictions is sometimes experienced in real life when we encounter psychological disturbance in others. In such cases, he wrote, the ordinary person has seen "the workings of forces hitherto unsuspected in his fellow-man but which at the same time he is dimly aware of in a remote corner of his own being."

In contrast to the uneasy responses of ordinary people to plagiarism, plagiarists themselves tend to be unequivocal. For example, modern scholarship has revealed that Edgar Allan Poe was a plagiarist—most dramatically in his book-length fiction *The Narrative of Arthur Gordon Pym*. Yet Poe himself regarded plagiarism as a "detestable" act and a "sickening spectacle." Similarly, Jacob Epstein, in his novel, treated a waffling response to plagiarism as a form of weakness. When the minor character, Professor Russo, who knows all about the "racket" of selling term papers, discovers that he has been handed two such papers, he ruminates, "Who the hell am I to set myself up as some moral paragon, as if I know right from wrong." Russo's failure publicly to expose his two student plagiarists is viewed by the narrator with contempt.

Plagiarists also tend to suffer from the delusion that they have been plagiarized from. Poe exhibited a perfect obsession on this point as with the subject of plagiarism in general. Over the years he collected materials for a book to be entitled "Chapter on American Cribbage," in which he planned to expose his contemporaries. His essay "Mr. Longfellow and Other Plagiarists" was full of wild accusations against some of America's most respected literary figures. The existence of a class of people, some plagiarists themselves, who spread false charges of plagiarism enormously complicates the problem, for the fear of being associated with false accusers often makes those whose work has actually been plagiarized from hesitate to say so.

Just as plagiarists differ from apologists in their moral attitudes toward plagiarism, so do they differ in being attracted to, rather than repelled by, the uncanniness of the subject. The scholar Burton R. Pollin showed that Poe, for his *Arthur Gordon Pym*, plagiarized from the travel book *A Narrative of Four Voyages*, by Benjamin Morrell. Unbeknownst to Poe, this book, which was actually in large part the work of a ghost-writer, contained many faked incidents. Uncannily, one might say, Poe relied "heavily" on the very material that Morrell and his ghost-writers had "borrowed." More recently, according to the *New York Times*, a writing instructor at San Diego State University belatedly discovered that a student had plagiarized the entire Janet Cooke Pulitzer Prize story about a supposedly unfortunate child: "Jimmy's World." Unaccountably—uncannily—the student had fastened on this particular story *before* it was exposed as an imposture.

Perhaps the most important and instructive case of plagiarism in English is that of Samuel Taylor Coleridge, who was first exposed as a plagiarist immediately after his death in 1834. During the next century and a quarter, a series of studies revealed that Coleridge had doggedly committed plagiarism from the beginning until the end of his career, in both obscure instances and in connection with some of his best-known and most influential works, especially those in literary criticism. Coleridge's stature as a poet is shaken, but not destroyed, by these revelations. This is because his reputation rests on a very few poems written over a short span of time. Although many of his other poems were plagiarized, his three great works—"Kubla Khan," "The Rime of the Ancient Mariner," and "Christabel"—cannot be called plagiarisms. But Coleridge's reputation rests almost equally on his literary criticism, most notably his *Biographia Literaria* and lectures on Shakespeare. And these writings contain particularly extensive plagiarism, including some of the passages for which Coleridge is most famous.

Surprisingly, it was not until the appearance of Norman Fruman's *Coleridge, the Damaged Archangel* in 1971 that any of this became a serious issue. Today the general reading public remains for the most part unaware that Coleridge was a plagiarist, while literary critics and professors of English—outside of those who specialize in the study of Romantic poetry—are largely unaware of the extent and significance of his plagiarism. The manner in which the present state of ignorance came about bears directly on the literary world's current unwillingness to deal with contemporary cases of plagiarism.

Norman Fruman's study reflected badly on scholars of Romanticism. Its information had long been available to them, as he pointed out, yet they rarely confronted it. Fruman remarked in the introduction to his book, "Except for a few lonely dissenters, the overwhelming majority of authorities in the field dismiss the charges of plagiarism and intellectual dependence against Coleridge as mistaken, or, at best, so partial a truth as to be grossly misleading."

Thomas McFarland was one such authority. His *Coleridge and the Pantheist Tradition* (1969) contained a chapter entitled "The Problem of Coleridge's Plagiarisms," which amounted to a compendium of scholarly defenses of Coleridge. Writing a short time before Fruman, McFarland observed that, in twentieth-century discussions of Coleridge, "there has been a curious and very widespread tendency to gloss over, and even to suppress, the fact of the plagiarisms." Nevertheless, he himself attempted to make the charge of plagiarism appear absurd, and he proceeded to cast aspersions on those who made it. His arguments, it is worth noting, have reappeared in the writings of apologists in connection with several recent cases of plagiarism.

McFarland's defense of Coleridge displayed an evident ignorance of typical plagiaristic practices. Thus, where Coleridge plagiarized from some of the very works that he mentioned, McFarland satisfied himself by asking rhetorically why Coleridge would be "determined to help his accusers by supplying the names of both the author and the book to which he is indebted." To be sure, this was before the appearance of John Gardner's book on Chaucer. But as a scholar of English Romanticism, McFarland should have known that earlier, in 1965, Albert Goldman, in *The Mine and the Mint*, had shown that Coleridge's contemporary, Thomas De Quincey, yet another plagiarist, had followed exactly the same pattern. In fact, Coleridge's case exhibited the typical anomalies of plagiarism—from guilt-ridden, self-incriminating gestures in the commission of the act, to a tainted exposer, to professional apologists, and finally to a highly moralistic attitude on the part of the plagiarist himself toward the very crime secretly being committed.

Coleridge—as McFarland noted—gave himself away "by using the words 'concealment' and 'plagiarism'" (a circumstance that McFarland found indicative of a confident innocence in Coleridge).

Furthermore, Coleridge devoted himself to accusations of plagiarism in others. "It is doubtful," Fruman wrote, "whether any other writer in the history of letters has accused so many writers of plagiarism, and so many so falsely." It was altogether fitting, therefore, that Coleridge should have been first exposed by another plagiarist, Thomas De Quincey, and that he himself should have entertained an honest affinity for the works of still another plagiarist, the Polish poet Casimir. Coleridge revered and openly imitated Casimir without suspecting what has only recently been revealed about him—that Casimir in turn had "'stolen *en bloc* and without acknowledgment from a contemporary Italian' the world-famous series of poems called the *Silviludia*." (Whereas Coleridge is known to have imitated Casimir, it is not yet known if he plagiarized from him as well.)

In McFarland's view, what called for analysis in Coleridge's case was not his plagiarisms themselves but rather the fact that a succession of nineteenth-century critics should have chosen to publicize them. He pointed out that several of the critics in question were Scottish, and theorized that their interest in the subject derived from "the traditional antipathy of the Scots toward the English." McFarland commented in particular on the exposures made by the Scot, J. C. Ferrier, regarding plagiarism in Coleridge's *Biographia Literaria*. McFarland wrote, "While on the one hand it is impossible not to be impressed by the relentless documentation of Coleridge's pilfering, on the other it is surprising and rather anti-climactic to find that when the firing is over Ferrier has discovered no more than nineteen pages of plagiarism in the hundreds that make up the *Biographia Literaria*." If nineteen pages are anticlimactic, it is not clear what would have impressed McFarland in the circumstances—twenty-one pages copied? Twenty-five? Fifty? Nor is it clear what McFarland would have made of Ferrier's case had he been, say, a Turk.

But the point is that McFarland was hardly alone in his tortured apologetics. When Fruman's book appeared two years after McFarland's, scholarly reviewers made no mention of their failure to have dealt forthrightly with Coleridge's plagiarisms. Instead, they dismissed Fruman for being "trivial" and "presumptuous." On the other hand, the same reviewers had to admit that Fruman's book was "formidably. . . well documented" (L. C. Knights), "thorough, well-written and well-documented" (Owen Barfield), and "carefully proofread" (Thomas McFarland, with perhaps a hint of regret). In the end, rather than deal with the case put by Fruman, these otherwise intelligent, even distinguished, critics preferred to accept the propositions that lack of need proves the absence of theft and that outright, unconcealed plagiarism proves the absence of plagiarism.

Inasmuch as these attitudes have spread out beyond the academy, it is worth recalling their intellectual origins in the Romantic doctrine of originality—a subject that has been of special interest to both Harold Bloom and Thomas McFarland. If the spectacular cases of Coleridge and De Quincey represented a kind of hysterical revolt against the tyranny of originality, then one can speculate on the phenomenon of sympathy for this revolt among modern specialists of Romanticism. Romantic refusal to be fettered by rules, it can be said, finds its modern equivalent in a relativistic questioning of the rules themselves by these specialists. In this perspective it makes sense that the scholar who wished the world free from the rigid certainties of Victorian moralism should have been Thomas McFarland himself. And it follows that McFarland should have gone on to conclude of Coleridge that "if translating some pages from his German contemporaries was his worst and blackest fault, then surely he was a prince among men."

At all times, to belittle a breach of professional ethics is to belittle one's profession itself. But in a period such as the present, when there is considerable doubt about the importance and dignity of humane letters, the refusal to render judgment has particularly unfortunate results. Today it is difficult to imagine a plagiaristic act, or indeed any other breach of literary ethics, that would go undefended. It hardly seems an accident that along with this particular devolution, literature, in general, went from a position where it could claim for itself the highest morality to one in which many are claiming that it is no more than a marginal entertainment.

A vendetta against plagiarists will hardly set things right again. The specific harms that plagiarism may cause are, after all, of far less importance than the act's threat to the moral climate of literature. It is therefore on this level that the problem should be addressed. Where there is an injured party, or where professional advancement over others has been gained through the employment of plagiarism, the issue must be brought out into the open. But where no one has been hurt, those privy to the circumstances, usually the plagiarist's colleagues and peers, ought to be counted on to inflict punishment enough with their personal disapproval.

Such an approach can be effective, however, only so long as the steady judgment of contemporaries and the objectivity of history can be counted on. While private judgment remains confused and scholars continue to treat literary wrongdoing as they have Coleridge's, there can be no confidence in the private handling of plagiarism. As long as such confidence is lacking, more and more cases are likely to be dragged into the courts and given wide publicity. Thus it is that the attempt to evade professional responsibility when a case of plagiarism arises only makes for further complications.

Ideally, plagiarism ought to be treated as one of those areas, like manners, where the enforcement of right behavior belongs to society at large. Given the present situation, it seems clear that literary critics and scholars must bear the responsibility to affirm that there is indeed such a thing as plagiarism and that they are capable of identifying it if necessary. When they come into contact with a charge of plagiarism, moreover, they must accept the responsibility to determine whether or not literary norms have been violated. With literary standards thus reasserted, it may become possible once again for the general opinion quietly to settle most cases of plagiarism by itself.

The American Scholar, Summer 1982

THE
DEMOTION
OF MAN

IN THE TWENTIETH century, the ordered universe broke apart into atoms, and man found himself alone. William Butler Yeats expressed the new sense of breakdown in a famous phrase, "the center cannot hold" (from his poem "The Second Coming"); it is at the heart as well of T. S. Eliot's "The Waste Land," surely the best-known modern poem, with its no less famous ending, "These fragments I have shored against my ruins." The American novelist Walker Percy, alluding to Yeats, recently summed up this conception, which has dominated the modern imagination right up to the present, in the following words:

> I think it fair to begin with the assumption, which seems fairly obvious, that, as the poet said, the center is not holding; that the consensus, while it might not have disappeared, is at least seriously called into question. Indeed, to judge from a good many contemporary novels, films, and plays, it often appears that the only consensus possible is a documentation of the fragmentation.

The lost consensus to which Walker Percy refers is one which stretched back, changes and permutations notwithstanding, for centuries. The Renaissance scholar E. M. W. Tillyard, in *The Elizabethan World Picture* (1943), describes the form it took in Shakespeare's time.

As epitomized in Ulysses' speech on degree in *Troilus and Cressida,* a great chain of being was imagined, extending vertically in logical, hierarchical steps from the highest to the lowest spheres of the universe. On the earth, rulers held sway over their subjects, fathers over their families, and man dominated the lower animals. The essential order of things was expressed in the harmonies of music and the rhythm and rhyme of poetry.

It was precisely the loss of this sense of order and authority that Eliot and Yeats mourned, a loss that found formal expression in the early twentieth century in musical disharmony and free verse. Yet if the twentieth century as a whole has been characterized by the conviction that we are living in a fragmented universe, the truth is that a coherent and ordered picture of the world has nevertheless gradually emerged and in the last decades has taken on definable form. The new picture is, in fact, modeled exactly on the old idea of an ordered hierarchical universe, except that the terms have been systematically reversed. Where once man was at the top of this order—only a little lower than the angels—now he is somewhere near the bottom; and where once his authority was taken to be divinely inspired and ordained, now it has come to be seen as a kind of usurpation.

The traditional justification for man's dominion over the earth, namely his superiority to other creatures, has now been challenged. After all, it is argued, animals, too, communicate and reason, they have emotions, and what is more they are on the whole less destructive than man. And as with animals, so with primitive man and with societies less developed than our own: both are closer to the sources of natural wisdom, and both wreak less damage upon the ecosystem and biosphere than does Western man.

By analogous reasoning, the earliest human societies, with their precapitalist forms of orgnization, are seen as the best. Here, unlike earlier attempts to celebrate the past over the present, which tended to favor the high achievements of classical civilization, the contemporary world view elevates the simplicities of past times. As for the future, that ultimate expression of the present, it is seen in the new perspective not as a hoped-for culmination but as a looming epoch of decline, a nightmare of overpopulation, cancer, famine, ecocide, nuclear winter.

The work of hierarchy reversal proceeds on many different fronts, and is undeterred even by such seeming obstacles as the Darwinian theory of biological adaptation, with its suggestion of progress upward to an apex that is man. "From a strict evolutionary point of view," writes one contemporary biologist, Bernard Rollin, "there is no top of the ladder, there is only a branching tree. If there is a 'top,' it has to do with adaptability and species durability and reproductive success. In that case, the rat shares billing with us and we both lose to the cockroach." The unfavorable comparison of man with cockroach has become a familiar staple of biological discussion—although Stephen Jay Gould is ready to take a stunning step even further down the scale:

> Evolution is a copiously branching network, not a ladder, and I do not see how we, the titular spokesmen for a few thousand mammalian species, can claim superiority over three quarters of a million species of insects who will surely outlive us, not to mention the bacteria, who have shown remarkable staying power for more than three billion years.

Here we have very nearly the ultimate demotion of man, the inferior not only of primitive peoples, other mammals, and the cockroach, but even of bacteria.

But there is still more—or, rather, less. It has remained for contemporary poetry to accomplish a fully imagined reduction of man beneath the status of cockroaches and bacteria. In his 1978 survey "How to Read the Contemporary Poem," the critic Paul Breslin points out that "the most popular key word in the new poetry" is "stone," standing for the "furthest things from the human—the least conscious, the simplest, the most innocent." What stones represent in the contemporary world picture may be gathered from an interview, cited by Breslin, with the Pulitzer prize–winning poet Galway Kinnell. "If you could go even deeper" on the contemporary scale, says Kinnell, "you'd not be a person, you'd be an animal; and if you went deeper still, you'd be a blade of grass, eventually a stone. If a stone could speak, your poem would be its words." Beyond this, surely, it is impossible to go, though if one considers the matter carefully enough, it is evident that there must be a reverse hierarchy among stones themselves, from the least valuable (diamonds, surely) to the most (perhaps the friable, vulnerable sandstone).

The strength of a world picture may be said to lie in its capacity to sustain itself in the face of contradictions. Thus, some lines written by John Donne a few years after the death of Queen Elizabeth indicate how it must have felt when the world picture of the time came under threat. Alluding to the philosophical repercussions of the idea that the universe might not be earth-centered, Donne observed that the

> . . . new Philosophy calls all in doubt
> . . . .
> 'Tis all in peeces, all cohaerence gone;
> All just supply, and all Relation:
> Prince, Subject, Father, Sonne, are things forgot.

Something like the confusion registered by Donne manifests itself (though not always with Donne's frankness) whenever our own contemporary world picture is threatened.

Of course, where post-Elizabethans were disturbed by evidence that the universe and the earth had not evolved in a harmonious fashion, those who hold the new view feel threatened by evidence of the opposite kind, and specifically evidence militating against the theory that the universe originated in a giant explosion—a big bang. This theory, suggesting chance and randomness as the underlying principles of the universe, supplies nothing that can be taken to ennoble man, and therefore offers satisfactions that are fully the equivalents of those the earth-centered universe of Ptolemy offered to the medieval and early-Renaissance minds. When evidence appears that would seem to contradict randomness—and in some fields, such evidence has been accumulating—it is routinely dismissed. In this respect, at least, the contemporary world picture is as efficacious as any that preceded it.

When it comes to geological history, chance and discontinuity have been wrung from the record with missionary zeal. Starting in the early 1970s, the mysterious disappearance of the dinosaurs came to be explained by a theory with negative implications for man in two ways. Purportedly, the dust from the crash of a meteorite, a sort of earthly big bang, blocked out the sun for a number of years, thereby depriving the dinosaurs of food. It could thus be concluded that man's survival as a species was due not so much to his adaptability as to the chance escape from catastrophe of his mammalian predecessors. At the same time, the prehistoric catastrophe served as a warning: through a similar blockage of the sun—this time in a nuclear winter brought on by the use of atomic weapons—man could bring about his self-destruction.

In 1985, however, paleontologists marshaled geological evidence that the extinction of the dinosaurs occurred over too long a period of time to be reconciled with a scenario of catastrophe. Then it emerged that most paleontologists—some 96 percent—had never credited the catastrophe theory in the first place, but had felt constrained to remain silent in the face of their opponents' moral fervor concerning the threat of nuclear war. To such an extent can the need to adhere to a world picture compromise scientific objectivity.

That the demeaning of man in the new world picture rests on a rather tenuous basis in observation has been repeatedly demonstrated by anthropological and ethnographic contretemps similar in their outlines to the fate of dinosaur catastrophism. The deciphering of the ancient Mayan hieroglyphs, for example, has made it possible to describe the life of that people, and incidentally to interpret the symbolic drawings accompanying their hieroglyphic script. The drawings turn out to depict a range of cruel tortures and self-lacerations. "Before going to war, for example," says a report in the *New York Times,* "the king would puncture his penis with a stingray spine, while his wife drew a thorn-barbed rope through her tongue." The Mayans were frequently at war,

> in large part to capture aristocrats for torture and sacrifice. If the Maya sacrificed humans in lesser numbers than the Aztecs, against whom they have often been held up as superior, they tortured their victims more viciously. Ancient ball games, like Roman gladiatorial contests, pitted captives against one another for their lives; the heads of losers were sometimes used for balls.

These discoveries are of interest both in themselves and for the light they throw on the scholars who have been surprised by them. As the *Times* reports, "Evidence of these darker practices has been available for decades in the Maya's stone reliefs and paintings," but scholars had explained it all away, interpreting the reliefs and paintings in such a manner as to place the Maya "on a mist-shrouded pedestal as austere, peaceful . . . students of the stars and the calendar." The pictures, in other words, functioned as virtual Rorschach tests, onto which their interpreters projected a collective wish to find in Meso-American prehistory an ingenious people at once gentle and mystical and accomplished in science and the arts.

Now that a rather different portrait of the Maya has emerged, a scramble is occurring to keep the bigger world picture in place. If, as the *Times* reports, the "new image" of the Mayans "is less romantic, it is also more human, scholars are quick to assert." Thus Professor David Friedel, an anthropologist at Southern Methodist University, believes that the self-laceration practiced by kings in advance of going to war in search of torture victims "indicates a cooperative, sacred relationship between the elites and the commoners." In other words, if the evidence shows a society's aristrocrats obsessed with self-mutilation and torture, a bit of interpretation will help us see beneath the surface to the class solidarity so characteristic of pre-Columbian America and so lamentably missing from the modern world.

To the north of the Mayans, the American Indians inhabiting what is now the United States fit into the new world picture as well—not so much exemplars of a superior civilization as object lessons demonstrating the defects of our own. The displacing of the Indians has long been a source of shame to enlightened consciences; modern historical accounts commonly include a broad indictment of the early American colonists and their descendants on this score. In the latest perspective, the actions of the colonists are often cited as examples of "exploitation" and "commodity capitalism," while Indians are portrayed as having lived in benign relationship with the land until introduced to anti-ecological practices by the whites. Such is the thesis of William Cronon's *Changes in the Land*, a recent, much-praised ecological history of colonial New England that has won the Francis Parkman prize of the Society of American Historians.

Yet here, too, the evidence has proved to be shaky. At least one scholarly reviewer of Cronon's book felt bound to point to "a body of evidence" showing that colonial agricultural practices did not rape and deplete the land, as Cronon has it, but rather were "carried on without plows, on fields that were fallowed far more frequently than he concedes." As for the Indians, "they burned the woods, some-times usefully but at other times more harmfully, and before moving on registered a heavy impact on the land on which their fields and villages were situated."

More interesting than this refutation, however, is the spirit in which it is presented. For the reviewer judges the book as a whole to be one "of impressive originality" and "penetrating scholarship," and he is at pains to assert that the factual refutations in his review in no way damage the book's thesis. After all, the "ultimate effect" of American settlement "was very much as Cronon has so brilliantly and provocatively described it." Thus, it does not matter whether an author is right or wrong concerning the period he has chosen for study, so long as he holds the approved view of modern civilization.

The effects of a scholarly orthodoxy on those who dissent from it can be seen in the case of Alden Vaughan's 1965 book *New England Frontier: Puritans and Indians 1620–1675*. Even before Vaughan's book appeared, a consensus had grown according to which, in Vaughan's words, the Puritans "appropriated the natives' land, bargained un-scrupulously for their furs, and abused individual Indians with im-punity." But Vaughan, starting out in perfect accord with this view, and wanting only to offer a more detailed account than any that existed for the earliest period of New England settlement, was sur-prised to find that "the evidence suggested a more humane and equi-table treatment of the natives." The Puritan colonists had "sought peaceful and equitable methods of acquiring land and furs, admin-istering justice, and recruiting converts": they had tried "to deal justly and peacefully with their Indian neighbors."

Although Vaughan's book was favorably received on its initial ap-pearance, it soon enough came under attack as its conclusions were increasingly seen to violate the orthodoxy of the time. In one dis-puted instance, that of the war between the Puritans and the Pe-quots, Vaughan's critics found not just that he was wrong in assign-ing blame to the Pequots but that the war was an act of Puritan "genocide." No matter that the Pequot tribe was not annihilated. No matter that here and elsewhere the historical record failed to support the charge of genocide. The Puritans, the new scholars declared, must have destroyed the relevant documents.

In the face of this assault, Vaughan was forced into retreat. In 1979 he brought out a revised version of his book in which he muted both his defense of the Puritan settlers and his exposures of Indian atrocities. Vaughan writes in his 1979 preface that on reflection he had overstated the case for the Puritans. And as for the Pequot war, "I am less sure than I was fifteen years ago that the Pequots deserve the burden of blame." Still, a careful reader will note that Vaughan never really yields on the substantive issues, and in his footnotes he makes it clear that the new historians have built their case on a misuse of scholarship. In the end, Puritan "genocide" turns out to be another catastrophe that never occurred—but also another scholarly article of faith to doubt which can be damaging to one's reputation.

Doubt of any kind has hardly affected the new world picture of primitive peoples and their virtues. In the early 1970s, for example, two primitive societies were discovered and presented to the world: the gentle Tasaday of the Philippines and the benighted Ik of Uganda. Both were much exploited in the service of demonstrating the degeneracy of civilization.

In 1971 a dozen natives and their children were discovered living in the rain forest on the island of Mindanao in the Philippines. In *The Gentle Tasaday*, John Nance, the reporter who first publicized the discovery, wrote in personal terms of the lesson these near-naked people teach to civilized man. As against "the popular image of Stone Age man, hulking and grunting, crude and dull," the Tasaday knew no cruelty or evil. They were ignorant of "killing, murder, war"; they did not so much as punish their children. When asked to describe evil, they replied: "We can't think of anything that is not good."

Charles Lindbergh, appropriately enough a member with Nance of the large, media-event expedition that quickly made its way to the Tasaday, expounded further on their significance for modern man. "The rise of intellect has coincided with the decline of natural life," Lindbergh explained. Technology, produced by intellect, has "taken us to a stage where life is endangered, man included. We are destroying our environment through pollution." For both him and Nance, the answer to this danger lay in the countercultural ideal of "touch and tenderness," epitomized by the Tasaday with their "simple beauty, their mysterious purity."

As it happens, the enthusiastic reception accorded to Nance's book revealed far more about the self-image of contemporary civilized man than was ever revealed about the two dozen Tasaday, who were only briefly visited before being cut off from the outside world. Nance, in fact, had himself originally set out to expose the early reports of the Tasaday as a hoax, perpetrated (as he then thought) by a flamboyant official of the Marcos government named Manuel Elizalde. Nance had been taken to the Tasaday under suspicious circumstances. Elizalde let him see the group only after he himself had gone ahead to meet with them, by his own admission arranging for them to remove their clothing and don orchid leaves, which he claimed to have been their authentic dress up until the time they were discovered. He then seated them on a log and finally presented them to Nance, who found their pose "too perfect." But at precisely this moment, Nance, flooded with awe, was converted from skeptic to apologist.

In retrospect, it becomes evident how much common sense had to be sacrificed in the service of this conversion. One notices now, for instance, that Nance's report of a "lack of serious health problems" among the Tasaday is belied elsewhere in his book by accounts of disease. And recently it has been said once again that the whole story of the discovery of the Tasaday may be fraudulent. Yet the wish to believe remains as strong as ever. Thus, when the *New York Times,* breaking a month-long silence, finally carried a report of the new charges of fraud, it restricted itself to the information that recent visitors, the first in ten years, had found the Tasaday wearing clothing and in possession of manufactured tools and other objects. "In interviews," the *Times* went on, "two anthropologists who recently revisited the tribe said these new possessions, which had aroused the skepticism of Swiss and German reporters who saw them recently, were an expectable product of the tribe's first contacts with outsiders in the early 1970s."

But why, if the Tasaday had come into extended contact with civilization in the early 1970s, should the Germans and Swiss have been surprised at the clothing? The answer, though one would not have learned it from the *Times,* is that the Germans and Swiss were not surprised at all. Instead, they reported being told by the Tasaday that Elizalde had "forced us to live in the caves so we could be called cave men. Before then, we had worn clothing, even though it was rather torn." The *Times* not only omitted this information, which was available to it as a subscriber to the Reuters news service, but also failed to mention that the two anthropologists interviewed for its own story were members of the original Nance expedition and deeply committed to the Tasaday story.

The "discovery" of the Tasaday, whether or not a hoax, seemed tailor-made to buttress the new world picture; by contrast, the mere existence of the Ik seemed calculated to undermine it, and to redress the balance in favor of civilization. The Ik were studied by Colin Turnbull, a professional anthropologist whose book on them, *The Mountain People,* appeared in 1972. As against the Tasaday, the life in nature of this isolated and primitive African group was one of unexampled Hobbesian viciousness. The individual Ik, whether adult or child, foraged strictly for himself. The group had failed even to establish a sufficient degree of community to arrange for the disposal of human waste, and as a result it lived in the unrelieved stench of human feces. Children were barely tolerated by their parents, and then only until they were three, at which point they were expelled from their homes. "Men would watch a child with eager anticipation as it crawled toward the fire, then burst into gay and happy laughter as it plunged a skinny hand into the coals." Virtually universal among the Ik were adultery, deception, cruelty to others and to one another. Far from protecting one another, "anyone falling down was good for a laugh . . . particularly if he was old or weak, or blind."

The implications of such a people for the romanticized conception of the primitive would seem all too clear. Yet Turnbull himself defended the Ik—on theoretical grounds. He concluded that they had probably once held to higher values—and "very likely" with greater fidelity than Western civilized men—but had had to abandon them "for the very good reason that in their context these militated against survival." The "context" Turnbull refers to is the severely deleted region the Ik inhabited, which itself had degenerated "with the advent of civilization to Africa." In other words, the conditions that produced the Ik were "a part of that phenomenon we so blandly and unthinkingly refer to as progress."

Turnbull goes even further, arguing that the Ik, "if we are honest," are not "greatly different from ourselves in terms of behavior." After all, starting with our kindergartens, and "reaching on through school and summer camps," we "effectively divorce" ourselves from our children. In fact, "there is not all that much difference" between us and the *animals*. "Technologically," Turnbull grants, "we are superior in some respects," but of course our technology is evil. And if it is true that we can speak—or as Turnbull grudgingly phrases it, if "we do seem to have developed the art of verbal communication to a point that gives us an enormous potential advantage over other animals"—here too "it can readily be shown that both speech and writing, misused, have led to many of the disasters peculiar to humanity." Much, indeed, can be readily shown, especially when the contemporary world picture is threatened as radically as it is by the horrors of the Ik.

Not surprisingly, Turnbull later was one of those who sprang to the defense of Margaret Mead when the methods and conclusions of her famous 1928 book, *Coming of Age in Samoa,* were challenged in 1983 by the Australian anthropologist Derek Freeman. Mead, it will be recalled, had depicted a Tasaday-like society which, thanks to unrepressed sexuality during adolescence, was virtually immune from such ills of modernity as rape and suicide. On the basis of his own investigations Freeman found to the contrary that the Samoans were not sexually unrepressed during adolescence but placed a high value on female virginity. Using court records and other evidence, he also showed that Samoan society displayed greater amounts of hostility than Western society, and had higher rather than lower rates of both suicide and rape. Turnbull, in his defense of Mead, avoided the scientific issue and instead praised Mead for her bravery and personal sacrifice—and her admirable criticisms of Western civilization.

An analogous defense has been mounted on behalf of those who, by attempting to teach sign language to primates, have challenged man on the grounds of his verbal uniqueness. In *Nim,* an account of one such attempt, Herbert Terrace writes that "until recently, humans could take comfort in the assurance that our language made us unique." Setting out to challenge that assurance, Terrace trained a chimpanzee named Nim for two years, teaching it to recognize numerous signs as well as to signal its wants.

As Terrace sat down to review his written and videotaped records, he had reason to believe that he had achieved a breakthrough. To his dismay, however, he discovered that neither Nim nor any other trained primate had used combinations of signs in genuinely sentence-like ways. Terrace came to this conclusion "reluctantly," and no wonder, given the hopes with which he had begun. Nevertheless, his was a rare victory for scientific objectivity.

The responses to that victory are another matter. The well-known science writer Martin Gardner, who accepts Terrace's conclusions, has pointed out that the desires of researchers have colored experiments to such a degree that an animal's failure to talk is often explained away as a joke or a lie. He cites Francine Patterson on Koko (made famous in the film documentary *Koko, a Talking Gorilla*):

> She asks Koko to sign drink. Koko touches her ear. Koko is joking. She asks Koko to put a toy under a bag. Koko raises it to the ceiling. Koko is teasing. She asks Koko what rhymes with sweet. Koko makes the sign for red, a gesture similar to the one for sweet. Koko is making a gestural pun. She asks Koko to smile. Koko frowns. Koko is displaying a "grasp of opposites." Penny [Francine Patterson] points to a photograph of Koko and asks, "Who gorilla?" Koko signs "Bird." Koko is being "bratty."

Though Gardner could not be more unequivocal in dismissing talking-animal claims, he himself, it is worth noting, declares a certain uneasiness at being put thereby in the company of the likes of Mortimer J. Adler (*The Difference of Man and the Difference It Makes*). Still, Gardner's uneasiness is mild compared with that of others, including Terrace's publisher. As Gardner observes, "nowhere on the jacket of *Nim* or in the book's advertising does the publisher so much as hint that the book severely criticizes practically all earlier work with talking apes." The publisher's silence was well calculated; in the event, one lone researcher has accepted Terrace's conclusions.

Today, Ursula LeGuin remains positively outraged at the "bad faith" of those who deny animal speech. She attributes their position to "speciesism," to "a need to believe in the unquestionability of human uniqueness, human supremacy." (Actually, the proclivities of Terrace and other critics lie exactly in the opposite direction.) Miss LeGuin holds in favor of animal speech despite several bizarre revelations that she herself recounts of eccentric, erratic behavior on the part of ape researchers. For example, Francine Patterson now keeps Koko "jealously and zealously guarded," and her results "have been so selectively released that even the most sympathetic scientists have trouble defending Miss Patterson's work." Another animal and its trainer "are keeping a low profile in the Pacific Northwest." Finally, almost unbelievably,

> Janis Carter, who worked in language experiments with the chimpanzee Lucy (raised as a "baby" by a couple who gave her to the training center), took her to an island in an African river, where the woman must live in a cage while two groups of chimpanzees roam free. Trying to free Lucy of her human dependence, Miss Carter will not use sign language with her.

Similar contortions in the service of the theory that animals are at least the equals if not the superiors of man have been undergone by Jane Goodall, the lady who lived "Among the Wild Chimps," as a *National Geographic* TV special had it. Goodall spent most of the years between 1960 and 1984 in close proximity to chimpanzees in the wild. She has concluded that they share essential traits with humans, including altruistic behavior, and in addition they possess a number of admirable and endearing qualities of their own. After fourteen years of study, however, Goodall observed something never before suspected of chimpanzees: they had begun to murder and devour their own kind. A mother and daughter became adept at seizing and eating the infants of other chimpanzees. There was no question of a food shortage, or of any resentment at work.

Goodall could offer no explanation for this unanticipated behavior—though a conclusion never mentioned by her or those reporting on her work is one that would have instantly sprung to the minds of scientists and amateurs alike in any period preceding our own, namely, that animals in their way, just as primitive peoples in theirs, exhibit behavior that is considered brutal by civilized norms. But to concede this would be tantamount to conceding the superiority of civilized man, an obvious impossibility. To anyone still foolish enough to hold such an idea, the usual retort is to point triumphantly to acts of torture, infanticide, cannibalism, and genocide committed by civilized societies themselves (while ignoring the fact that such violations of civilized norms have always been condemned as aberrations by the civilized world at large).

To remind us of our place in the scheme of things, the curators of the Bronx Zoological Garden in New York have thoughtfully positioned a mirror for visitors to the Great Ape House. Above the mirror is the legend "The Most Dangerous Animal in the World." Under it is written: "This animal, increasing at the rate of 190,000 every 24 hours, is the only creature that has killed off entire species of other animals. Now it has achieved the power to wipe out all life on earth." The curators, one understands, do not have in mind the American Indians—who joined civilized men in hunting the ivory-billed woodpecker until the bird was extinct on the North American continent. Nor are they thinking of the Maori, a South Pacific people who hunted the six-foot-tall land bird, the Moa, to extinction in New Zealand. No, the "animal" being referred to is the one from whose ranks came those volunteers in California who recently took turns supporting beached whales in their arms to enable them to breathe, not to mention the marchers in the 1984 All-Species parade in San Francisco who costumed themselves as crustaceans, birds, and trees to express their solidarity with forms of life ordinarily looked down on by man.

Most writers on these subjects are so committed to the relativist view that they routinely put quotation marks around the key terms of the discussion, "civilization" and "primitivism." The marks indicate that the writer rejects any tendency to elevate the one or to fail in appreciation of the other. "Cannibalism," too, regularly appears in quotation marks, both to indicate skepticism that it is as widespread as claimed and to allude to the view that "civilization" brings harms as great as or greater than primitivism. A note of irony often hovers about such quotation marks, as when Colin Turnbull distinguishes between "'advanced'" societies, which show signs of violent collapse, and "'backward'" societies, to which "this new violence has not yet come." Similarly, when he writes that the Ik have "'progressed'" to their present condition, he really implies that they have been the casualties of modern progress.

The vocal equivalent of such quotation marks can be heard in the tones of narration employed in television documentaries about animals and primitive peoples. The title of one of these, "Testament to the Bushmen," may stand for all, with their invariable presumption of a widespread and deplorable tendency toward feelings of civilized human superiority. His voice dripping with sanctimony, the narrator at once gently castigates the audience and renders homage to the rare, underappreciated values to be found among the peoples and species who have been photographed.

Interestingly enough, however, what we see on the screen is often a picture of destitution, disease, or blank despair. As a narrator intones the virtues of Masai tribal life, for example, the camera may be revealing naked children covered with sores and beset by cattle flies so persistent that the children have ceased to pay attention as they crawl over their open eyes. Or the Maori will be extolled for their devotion to art and respect for nature while the camera roams over ancient carvings depicting a people living in fortified villages and constantly at war.

In a film about Nigeria, a solemn respect is accorded to "traditional healers," long spurned by "orthodox [Western] medicine"; it is wrong, we are told, to think that "one is better than another," when what is needed between the two is "mutual respect." Without irony, the camera shows a traditional bone setter, who helps heal his patient by breaking a cock's leg; when the cock heals, the patient's leg will heal as well. With the mentally disturbed, we are informed, the native way in Nigeria is to keep them in village surroundings rather than exiling them to the indifferent confines of institutions. In the village, they are cared for by a traditional healer, who uses incantations and herbal concoctions. The camera now takes the viewer to the dirt area behind the healer's hut. Here sit approximately a dozen mental sufferers in a line (the camera shoots only in close-up, making it impossible to view conditions in the dirt enclosure or to see how many are held in it). Some of them are shackled, some drugged; all straddle a ditch; none moves.

At least one public-television documentary has taken an anthropological look at modern man using images compiled from a year of photographing at and near a single busy corner in Manhattan. People are shown crossing the street, often hurrying. Some are abstracted, few are animated. In one sequence, the corner is viewed from a rooftop high above, so that the people resemble insects in a hive. The camera lingers over those passers-by who seem upset, disoriented, even frantic. The narration? Modern man is lonely, unhappy. He lacks a sense of community, suffers from anomie. Not revealed is that the disturbed faces are those of released mental patients who mingle with the crowds in this particular neighborhood. When it comes to civilization, the accepting, embracing eye—the eye that looks benignly on the disposition of the mentally ill in Nigeria—turns suddenly censorious and judgmental.

This is not to say that there are no discriminations to be made *within* Western civilization; the new world picture has as many gradations as any previous world picture. But once the principle of reversal is understood, it is easy to arrive at the contemporary view on any number of matters. Simply elevate students with low grades and poor test scores, for example, over high achievers (the former are talented, the latter unimaginative). Find virtue in the criminal, stodginess in the law-abiding citizen. For the highest accolades, move quickly to what used to be thought of as the bottom of society: children and the insane.

Better yet, find a Caliban. In Shakespeare's *The Tempest,* the wise magician Prospero is accorded sway over the lower creatures and the lower mortal Caliban—or so the play has always been understood. As Richard Levin has shown, however, contemporary literary criticism has systematically turned the meaning of this play upside down. The first step was to argue that Shakespeare actually intended Prospero to be "equated" with Caliban in evil. Next, Caliban himself began to be viewed favorably. By the 1980s he "represented any group that felt itself oppressed." In one production of the play in New York, "he appeared as a punk rocker, complete with cropped hair, sunglasses, and Cockney accent." A feminist critic has imagined a soliloquy for Prospero's daughter, Miranda, whom Caliban once tried to rape, in which she concludes, "I need to join forces with Caliban."

In the Elizabethan world picture, man was constantly admonished to remember that his place was both high and low in the scale of things: above the animals but below the angels, possessed of reason but subject to the passions. "What a piece of work is a man!" Hamlet exclaims, but in the same speech calls him "this quintessence of dust." And Prospero himself, as Tillyard points out, calls Caliban "this thing of darkness . . . mine," as a reminder that his limitation as a human being is to be linked forever with the bestial. That this link should become a point of pride, that Caliban should be apotheosized rather than seen as a cautionary example—this is a development that could hardly have been predicted.

In the 1980s signs typical of a disintegrating world picture have appeared. Those clinging to the still-dominant, low view of man increasingly have resorted to the unverifiable to sustain their case, positing eons-old explosions in space, fanciful interpretations of prehistoric hieroglyphs, putatively destroyed documents, conjectures about the mind processes of inarticulate primates. When their slenderly supported metaphysical constructs are refuted, they respond with recriminations against the bearers of bad tidings. Still, some, like Herbert Terrace, have found that their first allegiance is to the scientific method, and in this there is hope. It now remains, just as it did, *mutatis mutandis,* at the time of the breakup of the Elizabethan world picture, for the implications of evidence favorable to man to be assimilated. The contemporary world awaits its John Donne: a poet capable of abandoning the comfort of stones in favor of the rigors of self-respect.

Commentary, September 1986

THE DARK AGE
OF THE
HUMANITIES

===

THE MUCH-DISCUSSED crisis of the humanities actually has two parts, the more serious one of which is the less noticed. First there is what might be called the traditional crisis. It goes back some thirty years, and has had to do with the dominance first of modern science and then of social science, with a consequent falling off of student interest in nonscientific and non-technical studies, with drops in literacy, and with diminishing knowledge of the past. This crisis deserves to be called traditional not only on account of its longevity, but also for carrying so many of the comforts of tradition: familiarity, venerability, rich resources for viewing with alarm (with a satisfying casting of distinction on the public speaker who bemoans the crisis), and above all the opportunity to solicit funds from charities and governmental sources. Money is always urgently needed for better academic instruction, additional courses in the humanities, institutes and endowments to further the cause of the humanities, and above all grants to study the crisis of the humanities. The decline of the humanities, in fact, correlates suggestively with the growth of subsidies for the study and cure of their crisis.

The second crisis has to do with the beneficiaries of the first: the nominal guardians of the humanities. These viewers with alarm—college presidents, foundation directors, members of institutes of the humanities, concerned educators, professors, deliverers of com-

mencement speeches, and testifiers before congressional commit-
tees—have succeeded in raising money to save the humanities. But
what they have in mind proves to be very different from what they
profess. They employ an apparently beneficent rhetoric to state their
intention, which is putatively to "revitalize," or "renew," or "reform"
the humanities. But their clichés of revitalization betray the presumption of an intellectual class confident that it has everything to
teach and nothing to learn from the past. What these self-appointed
saviors really intend to teach is that the usual assumptions about the
nature and use of the humanities are mistaken. Rather than a renewal, they have undertaken an undermining of the humanities.

To understand the program of the guardians of culture, it is useful to
recall how and when the assumptions they are challenging evolved.
The term *humanities* started out as a simple designation for secular
as opposed to theological studies. The idea of personal cultivation
gradually came to be associated with the study of these "humanities,"
and with the great revival of classical learning by the humanist scholars who made the Renaissance, the term came additionally to signify
love of the past, the elevation of man, and the spirit of free inquiry.
With the displacement of the basic building stones of the classics—
namely, the study of Latin and Greek—by the modern languages in
the late nineteenth century, the reason for being of the humanities
became unclear. For if their role did not inhere in the traditional subjects, which could be and were being replaced, their value had to lie
elsewhere, or not exist at all. Clearly a more philosophical definition
of the humanities was called for. This had been supplied by Matthew
Arnold in his description of literary study, by which he meant what
we could call the humanities. Literary study was an attempt "to
know the best that is known and thought in the world." This knowledge was to be pursued in a disinterested spirit, and its ideal result
was to be an improving and uplifting process. With Arnold's refine-
ment of the Renaissance ideal of the humanities the matter stood
right through the first, or traditional, crisis of the humanities some
thirty years ago.

The second crisis, a phenomenon of the 1980s, has arisen in part
out of attacks precisely on the Arnoldian definition and the assumptions behind it. Rejected by the new guardians of culture, in fact,
have been his very notions of "the best," of disinterested inquiry, and

of spiritual uplift. Anyone familiar with current academic fashions will recognize at work here the questioning, associated with French poststructuralist thought, of all normative values. Norman Cantor has assigned to poststructuralism, allied with Marxism and feminism, a dominating influence in the universities, and he has traced to them the decline of student enrollments in programs such as English and history. Whatever its role in humanities enrollments, poststructuralism may certainly be said to practice an *anti*humanism, pointedly displacing as it does the individual as the center of scholarly interest and the measure of sublunary things.

There remains considerable uncertainty over how far this antihumanism has progressed. At last year's Modern Language Association convention, Gerald Graff found exaggeration in Secretary of Education Bennett's publicly voiced fears that literary theorists were undermining the Arnoldian vision of the humanities. Not that the theorists weren't trying, Graff admitted. But he was confident that their ideas had not really penetrated very far. Graff was contradicted, though, by one of these theorists who happened to be sitting on the same panel with him. She herself explicitly repudiated Arnoldian humanism as an instrument of "capitalist hegemony." She expressed confidence, furthermore, that literary theory such as her own was on the point of triumphing in English departments. At another session of the convention, Professor Barbara Foley agreed. She described Marxism as triumphing in literary criticism, and she reported that in the university "subversion is the new order of the day."

What Barbara Foley seemed to have in mind can be observed at the administrative-operational level (or what might best be called the pundit level) of the universities. Here antihumanism has come to rule in a manner stunningly described by Roger Kimball in an account of a public symposium entitled "The Humanities and the Public Interest," conducted by the Whitney Humanities Center at Yale University. An outburst of sympathetic laughter from the academic audience at this event, reported by Kimball, reveals much about the second crisis of the humanities. The speaker was Jonathan Culler, professor of English at Cornell University and a prominent poststructuralist. He held up for ridicule a description furnished him by a dean who had invited him to lecture at St. John's College in Annapolis. There, the dean reported, the curriculum consists of readings from the "greatest books."

Professor Culler and his audience found this statement "quite risible," reports Roger Kimball.

For after all [Kimball writes], what did the good dean from St. John's mean by the "greatest books"? Only books written by "white Western males before 1900," of course, something that for Professor Culler seemed to demonstrate how parochial— not to say ethnocentric and sexist—his correspondent's notion of education must be.

Dismissed by the laugh at Yale, one may say, was the very core idea of the humanities, that is, a recognizable tradition of great works functioning as a uniting cultural heritage.

In place of this heritage, one panelist approvingly reported, we are experiencing a "collapsing consensus" about what constitutes the great books, and indeed what constitutes the Western tradition itself. The consensus has been undergoing a process of what the panelist called "decolonization." For him, the resultant breakup of tradition will be a positive development leading to a new "multi-culture." Insofar as the familiar works of the tradition will continue to be read, they will be examined from an adversary point of view. As a result of this approach we will all realize that the works of the Western tradition, rather than supporting a social consensus, are actually "inherently subversive"—a proposition with which Barbara Foley, for one, would enthusiastically concur.

How pervasive are such notions, one asks again? Well, as the audience response at Yale makes clear, they were incontestably the sense of this particular conference, organized by one of the humanities institutes set up in response to the traditional crisis in the humanities under the auspices of a great university. They were put forward not only by the self-proclaimed deconstructionist Jonathan Culler, but also by ordinary professors, and by A. Bartlett Giamatti, the president of Yale, and by Henry Rosovsky, the former Harvard University dean responsible for that school's much-heralded new humanities program. A single voice spoke out for the old idea of the humanities. This was Norman Podhoretz, who was invited from outside the academy to offer what could be no more than a temporary, token challenge to its antihumanist consensus. Virtually as a matter of course, Podhoretz's view was dismissed for sharing with Secretary Bennett's what was termed "intellectual fundamentalism."

In 1982 Professor Walter Jackson Bate of the Harvard English department was treated in a similar manner to Podhoretz and Bennett for betraying a similar allegiance to the traditional idea of the humanities. Bate's essay "The Crisis in English Studies," without making a distinction between the traditional and the new crises in the humanities, addressed itself partly to each. Quoting Douglas Bush's remark that "the humanities are always in crisis," Bate identified as the first cause of this crisis the increasing academic specialization that has taken place during the present century. He then moved on to what I would describe as the realm of the new crisis. Here he blamed recent formalist criticism, notably poststructuralism, for divorcing literature from life, specifically for having, as he put it, "helped to cut off approaches in the arts to large public issues and values." This was the worst that Bate had to say about poststructuralism. He did not identify it as being antihumanist, as do its own practitioners. He never deviated from a mild and gentlemanly discourse. Yet no matter how attenuated as a critique of the new crisis in the humanities, his essay stood virtually alone for years, and was much abused by those opposed to the Arnoldian conception.

The inversion of values whereby the guardians of tradition have gone from attempting to cure a perennial crisis in the humanities to fostering a far more serious one of their own is an amazing event in intellectual history. For it is not often that an intellectual class goes, within a period of ten or fifteen years, from calling itself one thing— in this case "humanist"—to virtually defining itself by opposition to that very thing.

Such opposition is recorded in a review of a recent book in which poststructuralism is applied to American literature. The reviewer, Daniel B. Shea, explains that for the author "humanism" is "a pejorative term he uses in the spirit of Derrida and J. Hillis Miller" (both of whom, it should be added, were associated with the English department of Yale University). The author being reviewed by Shea explains in the book itself that the purpose of poststructuralism is "to do battle with humanism." The French theorists like Derrida from whom this purpose has been derived tend not to name "humanism" explicitly as the enemy. But Michel Foucault has unequivocally expressed the wish that humanism might disappear. And his attitude toward humanism is evident also in the following passage, which is obviously intended as a repudiation of Protagoras's dictum that "man is the measure of all things."

> To all those who still wish to talk of man [Foucault writes] . . .
> to all those who still ask themselves questions about what man
> is in his essence, to all those who wish to take him as their
> starting-point in their attempts to reach the truth . . . to all
> those warped and twisted forms of reflection we can answer
> only with a philosophical laugh.

Just such a laugh went up when the great books about man were mentioned at the Yale conference on the humanities.

The new antihumanism, then, in its speed of transmission, its virtually total reversal of values, and its penetration all the way down to the administrative level of consciousness, has been comparable in impact to such an event as the overthrow of the Ptolemaic system of cosmology. Yet inasmuch as there has in fact been no Copernicus to overturn the contemporary world picture, the present scramble to adapt to the new, posthumanist outlook calls to mind instead the kind of impact that follows a totalitarian takeover of the state. Or better still, it recalls the period before a revolution when, as in France in the 1780s, the intelligentsia and that part of the nobility interested in ideas succumbed in advance to an insurgent ideology.

Like a class preparing for its own demise, wherever well-funded programs professing to save the humanities are in place, the present guardians of the humanities can be found at work "decolonizing" and otherwise overthrowing their humanistic heritage. In the glossy brochure put out by the Humanities Council of New York University, for example, the university's president, John Brademas, explains that "the humanities have kept alive our sense of common values," which he defines as "those standards, patterns of behavior, approaches and assumptions we all share as part of the human community." This is to say that whatever homogenization comes about when the attitudes and prejudices of the international "human community" are thrown together equals the humanities. Though the word *standards* has somehow crept into President Brademas's definition, it is evident that not standards but cultural relativism is what he has in mind for the humanities.

In its sixty-three pages the N.Y.U. brochure does occasionally touch on subjects actually having to do with the humanities, and some of these subjects, remarkably enough, are (or appear to be) distinctly Western. For the most part, though, the well-endowed Humanities Council has spent its money on non-Western subjects and on social and political themes quite outside any previous age's definition of the humanities. The council's lecturers are invited to speak on such matters as "The Catholic Bishops and the Shaping of Nuclear and Other Public Policies," and "The Future of Socialism in the Advanced Societies" (a very rosy one, one may guess), and "Nuclear Disarmament." The council's awards are given for the study of nuclear war. Its symposia and colloquia, too, concentrate not on the humanities but on "The Spanish Civil War," "Sex and Gender Studies," "War and Peace Studies," "Immigrant Mobility in New York," "Comparative Social History" (that is, working-class subjects considered from Marxist and quasi-Marxist points of view), "European-American Relations," "Law and Society," "Computers," and, yes, "AIDS."

In the council's brochure, somewhere between the "Festival of India" and such lectures as "Stones, Bones, and Behavior in Human Prehistory" (the latter presented at the "Humanities in Dentistry" program), there is a single "Colloquium on Ancient Civilizations." But far from being accorded its brief moment in the sun, the glory that was Greece and the grandeur that was Rome are here reduced to discussions of "dowries and bride price," "human sacrifice in antiquity," and "maritime trade at Ebla conducted through the port of Mari." From this choice of subjects one understands why the Program Committee of the American Philological Society, the organization of American classicists, recently voted against a proposal to invite Secretary Bennett to address them. Bennett's call for a return to the teaching of the classics, one of their number was reported to have said, "doesn't really represent what is of contemporary importance in our field."

Together, the trivialization of the classical tradition and the act of giving the West second place in humanities programs are intended as indirect attacks on the heroic ideal, on bravery, on loyalty, and on patriotism. More direct attacks are made on the tradition for supposedly demeaning women and condoning the oppression of the lower classes. Of course, something can be said in support of each of these charges. The chronicles of the ancient world display much that is to be regretted, to say the least. But it has always been thought that the humanistic legacy consisted of what had been *redeemed* from the ancient record—hence the *best* that is thought and known in the world. At present, in contrast, the very idea of a high civilization distinguishing itself by its art and philosophy is denounced as elitist and chauvinistic. More appropriate to our uses, presumably, are stones, bones, and the maritime trade of Ebla.

That it would come down to bones could hardly have been anticipated in the early days of the traditional crisis of the humanities. Certainly no such development was imagined by the authors of the 1964 Report of the Commission on the Humanities, the document that launched the National Endowments and other institutional responses to the traditional crisis of the humanities. The opening statement of the 1964 report called on "humanists" to provide guidance for their countrymen by imparting "whatever understanding can be attained by fallible humanity of such enduring values as justice, freedom, virtue, beauty, and truth." To the substantial and growing portion of the academic community for which everything is ideological and textual, this statement, if made today, would betray itself as an establishment's self-serving manipulation of terms.

"Such enduring values as justice, freedom, virtue, beauty, and truth"—let us examine each of these as it would be treated today, beginning with *justice*. Whose justice? The white man's? The slave owner's? Patriarchy's? Or is it the justice of Western imperialism? So much for justice considered ideologically. But the term must also be considered textually. The Critical Legal Studies movement influential at Harvard Law School and elsewhere tells us that legal definitions are nothing more than constructs enforced by interest groups. *Justice* is one of these falsely defined terms. The word can be employed only if it is placed within ironic quotation marks.

The next term is *freedom*. Freedom? A luxury reserved to the privileged minorities just mentioned. Next comes *virtue*, a problematic category in philosophy for much of the twentieth century. In academic speech and writing, the term *virtue* is no longer current. It may be employed in special circumstances, but never, we may be sure, as a term of approval. Finally we come to *beauty* and *truth*, as in Keats's "'Beauty is truth, truth beauty,—that is all / Ye know on earth, and all ye need to know.'" The literary critic will point out that it is not Keats who utters these lines but the Greek vase of his "Ode on a Grecian Urn." Since the equating of beauty and truth appears in a merely dramatic utterance, we need not take it seriously as an artistic and moral credo. In any case, we can add, Keats failed to foresee that beauty would come to be viewed as a time-bound aesthetic category. Modernism would come along to displace beauty from its central place, and postmodernism would replace it altogether with a category more suitable to its own sensibility: namely, "the ugly."

Should the contemporary literary critic be asked to draw a moral from Keats, he would begin by adducing the fictionality of all so-called truth in literature. The sociologist could add that his discipline shows many of our dearest-held, commonly accepted truths to be errors. The historian, in the meantime, has concluded that there is no such thing as truth in history. What we call history, moreover, is itself no more than a fiction to be treated in the relativizing manner of the literary critic. The feminist knows that the use of the word *truth* is phallogocentric—that is, it is presumed to reflect the rigid categorization of reality typical of patriarchy. And the poststructuralist, from whom the term *phallogocentric* was derived, agrees with the Marxist that for political reasons the concept of truth is a false one to begin with. "Truth" is to be understood as yet another hegemonic imposition employed by the powerful to enslave society.

In answer to the question of how pervasive the new attitudes have grown, then, it is enough to note that one has to go all the way back to 1964 to find a report on the humanities still willing to speak unequivocally and unselfconsciously of justice, freedom, virtue, beauty, and truth. It is true that Secretary Bennett has attempted to bring such terms back into currency. And in an article titled "Renaissance Time," Jeffrey Hart has equated Bennett's efforts with Dean Rosovsky's Harvard reforms and with a still broader responsiveness in the "educational establishment" to demands for a return to the Western tradition. As a result of these developments, Hart concludes, "we are heading for seriousness in higher education." But this is to miss the combination of contempt and rage that Bennett has elicited from the educational establishment for his anachronistic usages. For example,

Professor Richard Poirier's book *The Renewal of Literature: Emersonian Reflections* contains a particularly instructive response to Bennett. Dismissing Bennett's recent *To Reclaim a Legacy: A Report on the Humanities in Higher Education,* Poirier remarks that "in citing Arnold at the outset, it merely confirms how entirely predictable will be its assumptions about literature." Those assumptions—quite naive, one instantly gathers—include the conviction that literature serves social and cultural functions. It is indeed predictable that Bennett would think so—only slightly less predictable than Poirier's dismissive contempt. For him, Bennett's traditional approach to the humanities is "merely one more journalistic-political maneuver designed to obscure the failures in contemporary political-economic-social arrangements."

Yet the humanities are not in trouble, in Poirier's view. They are not in trouble because they have no social or cultural functions that they might be neglecting. Our mistake in thinking otherwise derives from what he patronizingly calls "the notion that the writing and reading of literature have a culturally redemptive power." Literature has no such power, he continues, because it is "troubled within itself." Far from sustaining us, literature "shows the futility of any perfervid quest for truth, values and exaltations." And far from supporting culture and society, literature only tries to "restore itself to some preferred state of naturalness, authenticity, and simplicity." Literature, in other words, *opposes* not sustains culture. It follows that the humanities are not in trouble since, except for a few Reaganites attempting to divert attention from the poor, most teachers can be counted on to render literature morally nugatory.

In my view Poirier is wrong about the nature of literature. His description of it as estranged from culture and society mistakes its radical testing of constraints for a rejection of constraints. In the end, the great works of literature are reconciled with society, just as we must be in life. Yet if I am right, how is it that literature has failed to reconcile Richard Poirier? And how is it that, despite the salubrious tendencies of the great tradition, an entire class of antihumanists has sprung up likewise to deny reconciliation with society? Such developments refute the belief that the humanities are somehow beneficial in themselves.

In an article titled "Scholarship versus Culture," Jacques Barzun has pointed out that "cultivation does not come automatically after exposure to the good things." "If I did," he points out, "orchestra players would be the most cultured people musically and copy editors the finest judges of literature." George Steiner has made a similar point about the art critic Anthony Blunt, whose exposure to culture did not prevent him from betraying his country. Earlier, it was Steiner who confronted us with an example that has come to be frequently cited. "We now know," wrote Steiner, "that a man can read Goethe and Rilke in the evening, that he can play Bach and Schubert, and go to his day's work at Auschwitz in the morning."

Steiner's words—they were recently cited by Sidney Hook in his Jefferson lecture "Education in Defense of a Free Society"—remind us that a familiarity with the humanistic tradition arguably in advance of all other nations did not prevent Germany from perpetrating history's worst barbarism on the world. As for the, on that occasion, more tender Italians, they had twice been the directest beneficiaries of the tradition, first during the Roman Empire and again during the Renaissance, which they themselves were instrumental in bringing about. Yet both times their society was marked by a violence—as often as not among the cultivated classes—no less legendary than their artistic achievements.

But if the guardians of culture cannot be relied upon, it may be asked, is it not possible that today's students will reject the cynicism of their teachers even as they have recently been rejecting their liberal and radical politics? And under such circumstances do not the great works of our tradition have a life of their own, managing by themselves to transmit something of their outlook and spirit? Trusting that this might be so, George Steiner has expressed the wish that we could go back to the simpler ways of earlier times. Instead of interpreting the works of our tradition, wouldn't it be marvelous if we could just read them together, possibly learning parts of them by heart? "Isn't it pretty to think so," as Jake Barnes says in the last line of *The Sun Also Rises?* But the truth is that not all the great works easily yield up their meanings. Their wisdom, their insight, their ideal beauty require an assault determined to wrest these prizes from them. Untutored, we tend to understand only as much as we already know.

Take the woman of my acquaintance, something of a provincial romantic, who had an unsuitable love affair. She found in *Madame Bovary,* that biting satire on her type, an inspiring romantic heroine. Much later, when nearly seventy-five years old, she reread the book and, as she observed to me, it struck her very differently. Over a quarter of a century too late, thanks to finally comprehending her own experience, she grasped the irony of Emma Bovary's delusions. Or consider the cultural revolution and the fate of utopian desires in the 1960s. The revolutionary passions of that period could have been illuminated by a treasure house of late-nineteenth-century novels on revolutionary themes. For example, the fanatic destructiveness of the revolutionary type is explored in Dostoyevsky's *The Possessed* and Turgenev's *Fathers and Sons,* the latter being also a revelation of precisely the kind of intergenerational conflict and continuity at issue in the 1960s. There were, in addition, George Eliot's *Felix Holt,* on the behavior of crowds; Henry James's *The Bostonians,* on sexual deviance and radical politics; Flaubert's *A Sentimental Education;* Joseph Conrad's *Under Western Eyes;* and finally James's *The Princess Casamassima.*

James's last-named, prophetic work takes an idealistic young revolutionary, Hyacinth Robinson, on a tour of the great cities of Western civilization, whose system he is pledged to overthrow, and one of whose artifacts he is pledged to blow up with a bomb. The monuments and works of art he views are presented as having often been the products of exploitation and even rapine—just as they are presented in humanities programs today. Yet in the end the young man cannot bring himself to destroy a part of what Western civilization has built up. His revolutionary confederates of course have no such tender concerns as his. Accounting to them for his reluctance would be something like answering the attacks on Western civilization at a humanities conference today. The response to such attacks, James's novel suggests, must issue not from preachments about the value and importance of the humanities, but from a conviction of inviolable allegiance to the past.

Yet who, despite the existence of an illuminating essay by Lionel Trilling making many of these points, had the presence of mind and the sense of tradition to invoke *The Princess Casamassima* during the 1960s? The lesson here, too, seems to be that in seeking to deal with the crisis of the humanities it is not enough to invoke the value of the tradition. In *The Idea of a University* John Henry Newman, taking Cicero as his authority, wisely insisted on separating the pure pursuit of knowledge from those social ends "solely contemplated by those

who would ask of me the use of a University or Liberal Education."
In the present circumstances, especially, we are best served by a lively
sense of the limitations of the humanities, in particular their limited
power to improve or even enlighten the individual, or to serve in an
emergency. We should keep in mind, too, the ease with which the
great works can be manipulated by hostile interpreters. Finally, we
need to recognize that we are in an exceedingly bad period for the
humanities: a period of antihumanism that deserves to be called a
Dark Age of the Humanities.

In the dark ages of Europe after the Roman Empire, the danger to
the humanities had to do with the destruction and neglect of the
great texts. In our own dark age, the texts are suffering from the
wrong kind of attention. They are being subjected to a system of interpretation that is extinguishing their spirit quite as effectually as if
they were again literally under assault by Vandals and Goths. We are
probably not in a position to wrest the tradition back from its antihumanist interpreters, at least for the time being. But there are some
things we can do while awaiting another Renaissance. We can, to begin with, assess and offer a critique of the inflated rhetoric in which
the humanities are discussed by their traducer-guardians. In place of
their bombast we need to offer a true account of how humanistic culture functions and what it can accomplish. Claiming less, we may be
in a position to achieve more. Speaking modestly and acknowledging the frailty inherent in an intellectual and artistic tradition, we will
be in a position better to advise ourselves about its protection.

The minimal rather than the usual maximal case for the humanities may be stated in a single proposition. It is this: our predecessors
thought and expressed some things in ways that cannot be improved
upon. The proposition, minimal as it is, has the merit of being invul-
nerable to the most determined of deconstructivist interpreters. For
the proposition bypasses such questions as whether or not Iago is
evil—questions that throw open works of the past to modern interpretation, which has in fact produced defenses of Iago. Instead,
under the proposition Shakespeare's portrait of Iago would be recognized primarily for being a definitive one. In a similar way, the
starting point for discussion of Oedipus or Narcissus would be their
having captured certain human truths for all time. And so, too, with
the discussions of goodness and truth in Plato's *Republic* and the

Theaetetus: these would be seen as not-to-be-replaced starting points for all later discussions of these matters.

Much else follows from the minimal acknowledgment that the past cannot in some respects be improved upon. But first it should be admitted that if some of the achievements of our predecessors are unsurpassable, it nevertheless stands to reason that we *can* match many of them. Why should we not, then, replace the works of the past, when possible, with contemporary versions in more accessible styles? Why, indeed, have we ever preserved and why should we continue to preserve the humanities? The answer to this question, like Cardinal Newman's answer and like Henry James's in *The Princess Casamassima,* is not a practical one. Instead it derives from a sense of appropriateness toward the human record. It seems appropriate and fitting, though not necessarily practical, to preserve certain cultural artifacts. Once a truth has been expressed, or a work of art created whose quality cannot be improved upon, we sense that it should be allowed to stand.

This sense about works of the past, I would argue, arises from a profound instinct of race survival so that, after all, it does prove to be practical. It recognizes that the wish to be remembered amounts to a secular substitute for divine immortality, without which life rings hollow, and that such an ambition is possible only where there is an assurance that society will preserve its records, which prominently include the humanities. Thus the commitment to preserve these works amounts to a message to our children that in the future they may hope that whatever works they create will not be swept away so long as the culture values something more than the present. It behooves us to guard what was, we are telling them, so that those who come after us will guard what now is.

From the same assurance other benefits flow as well. First, he who would leave a mark on society is likely to conceive an interest in the preservation of society—no small achievement in our day. Second, he who recognizes what might be called the precedence of the past— its having already thought our thoughts—is likely to be rather skeptical about startling departures from social and cultural norms. In politics such a person will tend to be anti-utopian—another distinct gain. Third and last, he who has some sense of the achievements of the past begins to have a sense that there is something more appropriate than our evaluation of it, and more important than anyone's attempt to "deconstruct" it. This something is the way in which the past begins to measure *us*. It follows that for those who recognize this measuring function, the past becomes a kind of superego or restraining influence.

All three benefits—the wish to preserve society, becoming skeptical of departures from its norms, and feeling more judged than judging of the past—flow naturally from the idea of precedence. It is only with the introduction of interpretation as a method of instruction that the past can become subject to co-optation by the ephemeral purposes of the present. Interpretation by the individual cannot help taking place, to be sure. But when uninfected by oppositionist ideology, private interpretation will never on its own develop the antihumanistic bias so pronounced in our present intellectual establishment.

My reliance on the individual reader, though, brings us back to George Steiner's extreme case of cultured barbarism and its challenge to the efficacy of tradition. In response to Steiner it seems best to make another minimal though by no means insignificant claim. It is that the shock one experiences when presented with Steiner's killers actually tells us something positive about the humanities. For our greater shock at this than at other examples of the same barbarism comes from a dashing of our hopes for art, which we thought of as ameliorating evil in human nature. Steiner's example make us see that though art may not ameliorate evil, we continue to believe that its essential tendency is toward the good. Because we believe in this tendency, we view Steiner's cultured killer as if possible even more guilty than others who committed the same crimes. This belief, which itself constitutes a civilized value, also provides the best reply to the challenges of the now triumphing antihumanists: in the final analysis the tradition will judge us, and not we it.

In his *History of Classical Scholarship from 1300 to 1850*, Rudolph Pfeiffer describes three periods in which the classics and the classical spirit were recovered: in Alexandria, in fourteenth-century Italy, and in eighteenth-century Germany. Each time, poets felt a need to revivify language and literature by restudying the ancient texts. And each time their enthusiasm carried over into the culture at large in the form of a renaissance. In our own time not only has the classical tradition lost its authority, but also contemporary literature is desperately in need of revitalization. "In a dark time the eye begins to see," wrote Delmore Schwartz. In a dark age one is at least permitted to see clearly what is being lost by hostility to the humanities. And thanks to this clarity, one is reconciled to playing the only role that is truly respectable in a dark age: that of a curator of values. A renaissance cannot be mandated, but it can at least be prepared for.

Intercollegiate Review, Fall 1987

EPILOGUE

THE ACADEMIC
ASSAULT ON
ALLAN BLOOM

═══════════

UNLIKE THE POPULAR reviews
of *The Closing of the American Mind*, which were mixed, most of the
reviews by academics were hostile. In addition, Allan Bloom was contemptuously dismissed at academic symposia on his book; Clifton R.
Wharton, the former chancellor of the State University of New York,
called him an "elitist" and "racist"; and David Rieff, writing in the
(London) *Times Literary Supplement*, in addition to contemptuously
comparing him to John Wayne and Oliver North, declared that "men
like Professor Bloom . . . publish books decent people would have
been ashamed of having written." It is understandable that academics would react angrily to a book exposing the politicization of teaching and scholarship with which they have been associated in recent
years. And it should come as no surprise that their attacks, when not
simply abusive, also prove to be political.

Avoiding the critique of college education in the early and late
pages of *The Closing of the American Mind*—the portion of the book
that absorbed its popular reviewers and most readers—the professors concentrated on the long and convoluted middle of the book.
Here Bloom treats not education proper, but what he regards as the
roots of its debasement in the Enlightenment and in nineteenth-
century German thought. His critics denigrate the scholarship that
he brings to this task, and it has to be said that in certain of its details
their attack is damaging. But of far greater importance is the way
each of them also launches an attack on Bloom as an antidemocratic

elitist. For in doing so they raise questions about their own values far more disturbing than the imperfections of Bloom's scholarship.

Their strictures largely come down to the observation that Bloom fails to indicate the degree to which his interpretations of philosophers are debatable, especially if one prefers to stress historical context and the varying interpretations of other readers over time. From this point of view, too, Bloom is charged with failing to define his terms and for using philosophical categories imprecisely and even incorrectly. In addition Bloom has been faulted on stylistic grounds for an "unforgiving disorganization" and for a self-indulgent use of the subjective "I." Conservative critics Jeffrey Hart, Michael Levin, and Albert Weeks—all of whom support Bloom's view of education— are in agreement with liberal critics such as Martha Nussbaum and Peter Pouncey that these are the weaknesses of *The Closing of the American Mind*. Ironically enough, as the radical critic Michael Hays pointed out at a symposium on Bloom at Dartmouth, the characteristics of discontinuity observed by the critics make the book "a thoroughly postmodern text," that is, one which many of its liberal critics should admire. But in any case, it is fairly evident that scholarly and other weaknesses are not really the major concern of Bloom's critics.

Without excusing Bloom, it can be pointed out about these shortcomings that he does not present himself as a philosopher but as a teacher of humanities who has written a book of observations and experiences. These tend to read like transcripts of spontaneous classroom lectures. And whereas it is usually better in a classroom not to confuse students with scholarly disagreements but instead afford them a first-time, direct confrontation with philosophical ideas, he should have recognized that such an artificially pure confrontation is not usually appropriate for a book. Nor, strictly speaking, is Bloom's treatment of the philosophers Locke and Nietzsche, toward whom his attitude is distinctly ambiguous, appropriate for a book. Again, whereas it is sometimes well that students should at first not quite penetrate the professor's point of view, the writer of a book is under obligation to declare himself.

This is not to say that Bloom fails to make clear his view that Nietzschean nihilism, along with Lockian distrust of reason, is a crucial source of the relativisim presently troubling the academic world. But Nietzsche in particular functions in *The Closing of the American Mind* virtually as a Miltonic Satan, carrying a philosophy at once attractive and sinister, and alternately evoking Bloom's admiration and rejection. As a result of his ambivalent style of presentation here and elsewhere, Bloom has laid himself open to at least one spurious line of criticism as an elitist. This is the contention that he puts his faith in a few classic texts as a cure-all for the problems of the university. Actually, as his favorable critic David Gress, for one, has pointed out in the *New Criterion,* Bloom has no such confidence in the teaching of the classics. On a careful reading, one discovers that he finds all of them to be in some degree subversive—very much in the manner of Locke and Nietzsche.

Bloom's vivid diagnosis of the flaccid, closing mind of the American university, then, though it has understandably strengthened the hand of those who would defend the classics, is accompanied by a darkly hermetic vision. Classical studies may benefit the individual, but they foster a kind of skepticism dangerous to the state. Nor would Bloom have it otherwise. For he believes that history teaches the folly of trying to foster ideas or attitudes likely to benefit one's country. When in the past philosophy has thus stepped outside its proper realm of pure thought, even with the best of intentions it has made itself subject to politics and politicians, he argues. And this can lead, as it did in the case of the German philosopher Martin Heidegger and others, to support of an evil regime such as that of the Nazis.

Ignoring this fear, Bloom's critics have seized on his assignment of an insulated and elevated role for philosophy as evidence of a distaste for the democracy in which he lives. The major essay reviews attacking Bloom in this manner are by Benjamin Barber of Rutgers in the *Atlantic,* Alexander Nehemas of the University of Pennsylvania in the *London Review of Books,* Martha Nussbaum of Brown in the *New York Review of Books,* and Richard Rorty of the University of Virginia in the *New Republic.* All of them judge Bloom to have rejected not the union of philosophy and the democratic state but democracy itself. Barber's essay, titled "The Philosopher Despot," pronounces Bloom "profoundly anti-democratic." Martha Nussbaum condemns "Bloom's final rejection of democracy, and of the democratization of philosophy." Richard Rorty tries to strike a lighter tone, referring to "an admirably frank expression of doubts about democracy" on Bloom's part. But though Rorty delivers his critique playfully by referring to things he *could* say—"I could easily go on about intellectual snobbery, failure to trust the Healthy Instincts of

the People, and of course, 'elitism'"—all of these are obviously inte-
gral parts of his critique.

For all of these critics the source of Bloom's elitism is his prediction that few will ever join the charmed circle of those who intimately involve themselves in the eternal philosophical issues. Because
of this prediction Nussbaum stigmatizes Bloom's philosophy as "the
preserve of a narrow elite." In her view he equates those students
who may be expected to join the circle with the wealthy who are
privileged to go to Ivy League and other elite colleges. Barber, using
italics to strike what can only be described as a tone of piety, writes
that Bloom "elevates the few over the *many* who embody America."
Delivered as denunciations rather than in the form of argument,
these caricatures of Bloom have the evident purpose of discrediting,
not refuting him.

An attempt at refutation, in contrast, would soon expose an underlying confusion on the part of these critics between political democracy and the adoption of democratic procedures outside of government. Being a democrat has to do, properly speaking, with support
of a democratic system of government. One does not become either
more or less democratic by advocating or opposing democratic procedure in other contexts. Nor is political democracy enhanced by
democratic social behavior or equalitarian educational practices. The
president of the numismatic society who rules with an iron hand is
not thereby any less a political democrat than the president of the
philatelic society who governs by referendum, nor is the democratic
state within which both operate enhanced by the one or demeaned
by the other.

The notion that the attitudes and practices of people in a democracy should have a democratic cast was nicely observed by John
Adams when he was ambassador to France during the American
Revolution. Writing in his diary in 1783 he observed that every political system has its peculiar "demon." In France, he observed,

> the demon of monarchy haunts all the scenes of life. It appears
> in every conversation, at every table, and upon every theatre.
> These people can attend to no more than one person at a time;
> they can esteem but one; and to that one their homage is
> adulation and idolatry.
> I once heard the Baron Van der Capellen de Pol say, that

the demon of aristocracy appeared everywhere in that republic
[i.e., the Netherlands, which Adams classified as an aristoc-
racy], that he had collected together a number of merchants
to sign a *requête;* they agreed upon the measure, but insisted
upon appointing a committee to sign it. Many of them declared, they would not sign it with a crowd—*avec une foule.*
Thus it is that the human mind contracts habits of thinking
from the example of government; accustomed to look up to a
few as all, in an aristocracy, they imitate the same practice in
private life and in common things; accustomed, in monarchies,
to look up to one man in great affairs, they contract a similar
disposition in little ones.

   In the same manner, in democracies, we contract an habit of
deciding every thing by a majority of votes; we put it to vote
whether the company will sing a song or tell a story. In an
aristocracy, they ask two or three of the better sort; in a mon-
archy, they ask the lady or the gentleman in whose honor the
feast is made.

Adams did not refer to a democratic "demon," but in our time, in the
academic world, surely that demon can be found at work in promiscuous charges of "elitism."

   Underlying these charges is the fallacy, pointed out by Harvey
Mansfield, Jr., in a rejoinder to Richard Rorty in the *New Republic,*
that an attack on Bloom for elitism "implies that the right elite is
closer to the people than the wrong one, hence [is] not really an
elite." In other words, Bloom's academic critics represent a highly
selected special class no matter what their attitude toward elitism
may be. The delusion that it could be otherwise, it can be added, is a
peculiarly democratic one. Only in a democratic society, one suspects, could there arise the phenomenon of academic anti-elitism:
that is, the conviction held by an elite professoriate that by virtue of
espousing democratic-leveling tendencies they cease being an elite.
In this vein Benjamin Barber, pronouncing Bloom an elitist, invokes
a kind of elite-eliminating magic by associating himself with "just
plain folks," as he phrases it, and by referring to "we citizens" (implying that the phrase could not possibly apply to Bloom because of
his opinions).

   Ironically enough, Bloom's critics prove not only to be members of an elite in the sociological sense, but also to hold at least one opinion about education far more elitist than any of his. This becomes apparent when Martha Nussbaum locates Bloom's heresy in his putative indifference to "the diverse needs of diverse groups of American students." She does not specify which groups she has in mind or what their needs might be, but she is clearly implying that where Bloom would reach only a few students she would reach the many. As for the students' "diverse needs," it is fairly evident that she is not expressing concern for the wealthy and privileged whom she has accused Bloom of preferring. Instead she appears to have in mind ethnicity, race, and lower socioeconomic status, and to be implying that these posit special educational needs. And though the needs are not specified either, it is also fairly evident that Nussbaum is not implying that Hispanic students, for example, require more Greek philosophy or should read more of Shakespeare's plays than other students. Obviously, she is advocating specially tailored, lower-level instruction according to race, ethnicity, class, and presumably gender.

Now let us compare Bloom. He would expose all students to the same curriculum of Western classics, expecting, as noted, that only a few would grasp these works in their full depth. Benjamin Barber admits that Bloom allows such access to all students "in principle," but complains that "in fact this includes only a few," as if the outcome somehow compromises the principle. But so long as the opportunity to become one of the few remains open to all there has been no such compromise. Surely choosing in advance who will and will not be exposed to the full range of the difficult great works is not more democratic than this.

Nussbaum nevertheless attempts to validate her approach by sentimentally associating it with what she describes as the "genuinely democratic" alternative to Bloom found in a 1945 report on education. This report, presumably like Nussbaum herself, is said to evince an "evident affection for the entire country of diverse people whose education it proposes to discuss." Democracy is here supplied by the ethic of caring. (Benjamin Barber takes the same tack, substituting "compassion" for Nussbaum's "affection." Both usages call to mind Bloom's Veblenian phrase "conspicuous compassion.") The implication is that if you *care,* then you are free to impose an invidious preselection of subjects on students—deciding their educational options for them according to the circumstances of their birth—and this action will be democratic by definition.

But these critics' talk of caring and compassion seems calculated not only to lend themselves a democratic aura but also, and more importantly, to delegitimize Bloom. He is said, for example, not to love the democracy which they in particular embody. In contrast, Richard Rorty claims that unlike Bloom his party "can deal honestly with the public." Furthermore, "we do not let the institutions of society humiliate those whose tastes and habits we find contemptible." Here Rorty raises up the demon of democracy, and its visage displays precisely what Socrates, Plato, Aristotle, and Cicero identified: the demagogic temptation. This consists in encouraging abuse of an opponent by depicting him as more or less an enemy of the people. That is the effect of implying that Bloom, the very soul of whose intention lies precisely in an utter separation of philosophy from politics, would rule popular taste through some kind of political action.

The truth is that rather than being defenders of the people at large, these demagogic critics are partisans of one party in particular. So much is clear from the way in which they allow respectability to a single political attitude. What this attitude must be and which party represents it is never explicitly stated, but these things can be gathered readily enough from passing remarks by Nussbaum and Rorty. The former, for example, writes that Bloom "actually despises the search for social justice," while the latter congratulates himself (yet again) that unlike Bloom he is among those who look for "some concrete proposals for the reform of American institutions." Is it heretical, then, to believe that American institutions are not, generally speaking, in need of "reform," or to believe that social justice is not something that remains to be found and duly acknowledged in the land? Doubts about both of these needs, after all, have been evidenced by American voters (the democratic majority) in recent years. Of course such doubts are hardly countenanced by many within the American academy, where the tendency is to identify democracy with the left wing of the Democratic party.

Following de Tocqueville, Bloom greatly fears the promiscuous extension of democratization into every issue or controversy. He therefore conceives himself as having a role akin to that of Socrates, the gadfly of the Athenian polis. But whatever Socrates might say about American representative democracy, Bloom himself is certainly not disposed to attack it, though he should have a perfect right peaceably to do so if he should wish. On the contrary, his support of democracy is manifest in his saying that "in an aristocracy the university would probably have to go in a direction opposite to the one taken in a democracy to liberate reason." This is not to advocate an aristocratic party line in democratic universities, but rather to suggest that democracy is best served when the universities encourage critical-mindedness and other forms of cultivation which are "aristocratic" in a nonpolitical sense.

Democracy is worst served, one may add, by the kind of demagogic appeal resorted to by Bloom's critics. For in setting loose the demon of democracy, they call to mind de Tocqueville's description of what happens when the democratic majority is raised up to omnipotence. "I know of no country," de Tocqueville writes,

> in which there is so little independence of mind and real freedom of expression as in America. In any constitutional state in Europe every sort of religious and political theory may be freely preached and disseminated; for there is no country in Europe so subdued by any single authority as not to protect the man who raises his voice in the cause of truth from the consequences of his hardihood. If he is unfortunate enough to live under an absolute government, the people are often on his side; if he inhabits a free country [i.e., a constitutional monarchy], he can, if necessary, find a shelter behind the throne. The aristocratic part of society supports him in some countries, and the democracy in others. But in a nation where democratic institutions exist, organized like those of the United States, there is but one authority, one element of strength and success, with nothing beyond it.

Bloom's critics would represent him to the one authority of the democratic state—the majority—as an antidemocrat, and thereby make him an outcast.

For Bloom the danger of mixing politics with philosophy is so great that he advocates a retreat to the ivy tower. He thereby renders himself easily caricaturable as a self-indulgent elitist. As an alternative to absolute separation between politics and philosophy, one of his conservative critics, Charles Kesler, writing in the *American Specta-*

tor, has expressed confidence that the philosophical issues can safely be put to the people in a democracy such as our own. Kesler believes that the civic humanist spirit will prevail over mob instincts, and it must be said that something like this certainly seems to be confirmed by the thoughtful popular reaction to *The Closing of the American Mind.* On the other hand, Bloom's liberal and radical critics have done nothing to support such confidence. In succumbing to the demagogic temptation in their attacks on him they have gone a long way toward confirming his skepticism about the American mind.